THINK BIGGER!

By T.J. Rohleder
a.k.a. *America's Blue Jeans Millionaire*

BE SURE TO CHECK OUT OTHER GREAT TITLES FROM THE **BLUE JEANS MILLIONAIRE LIBRARY:**

The Magic Pill
The 2-Step Marketing Secret Than Never Fails!
The Wow Factor!
3 Steps to Instant Profits!
Instant Cash Flow!
Money Machine
The Power of Hype!
Stealth Marketing
Jump... And the Net Will Appear!

TABLE OF CONTENTS

Introduction:

By T.J. Rohleder

THE TWO THINGS THAT CAN MAKE YOU MORE MONEY!

Thank you for purchasing this book and taking the time to go through it. This was a wise decision on your part. As you'll see, the information inside this book can make you huge sums of money! Nowhere is that MORE TRUE than in the first chapter, which gives you the secret to making more money by...

THINKING BIGGER!

This is the FIRST secret to making the most money in your business. **You simply must THINK BIGGER than all of the other people you are competing with.** You must set bigger goals and get a bigger vision for yourself and your business. And as I tell you in the first chapter, you must be willing to do the things that others are NOT willing to do.

Expanding the size of your thinking is not a guarantee that you'll make more money. Sorry. Some of the biggest thinkers in the world are dead broke or sitting in some insane asylum right now. In fact, many of the world's most delusional people are BIG THINKERS who must be protected from themselves and others!

THINK BIGGER!

But when you mix BIG THINKING with SOUND MARKETING AND BUSINESS PRINCIPLES — you have the awesome power to make more money than you've ever dreamed possible! So that's the SECOND thing you need to make huge sums of money. And that's where this book can help you a great deal.

In a nutshell, just use the methods in Chapter One to EXPAND YOUR THINKING and then channel it in the most powerful ways by using the rest of the secrets in this book. These other secrets have to do with something that can make you enormous sums of money in any business...

Marketing And Innovation.

Marketing is made up of all the things you do to ATTRACT and RETAIN the very best customers in your marketplace. These customers are vital to your success. Here's the simple formula for you to channel your expanded thinking around: **Just get enough customers to repeatedly give you more of their money... more often... and for more profit per transaction... and you can make more money than you've ever dreamed possible!**

Yes, it all starts with the BIG VISION that you'll get when you apply the secrets in Chapter One. So please study this chapter carefully and begin to use the methods at once! And then go through the rest of this book and study the specific marketing methods that I'll give you and **FOCUS ALL OF YOUR ENERGY into using those methods in the biggest way.** Do this and you can make all the money you want and need!

So begin today! Go through the first chapter very carefully. Think deeply about the awesome power that thinking bigger can give you. Then use it with the other powerful marketing ideas and methods you'll discover throughout the rest of this book. **DO THIS and you'll be on your way to making all the money you want, need, and truly deserve!**

And to reward you for purchasing this book, I have…

A great FREE business-building gift for you!

Yes, I have a gift waiting for you that can DRAMATICALLY INCREASE YOUR SALES AND PROFITS! Here's what it's all about: I spent TEN FULL YEARS writing down all of the greatest marketing and success secrets I discovered during that time period. Each day, I took a few notes and, at the end of a decade, I had a GIANT LIST of 6,159 powerful secrets! This list is ALMOST 1,000 PAGES of hardcore money-making ideas and strategies!** **Best of all, this massive collection is now YOURS ABSOLUTELY FREE!** Just go to: www.6159FreeSecrets.com and get it NOW! As you'll see, this complete collection of 6,159 of my greatest marketing and success secrets, far more valuable than those you can buy from others for $495 to $997, is absolutely **FREE.** No cost, no obligation.

Why am I giving away this GIANT COLLECTION of secrets that took ONE DECADE to discover and compile— FOR FREE? That's simple: I believe many of the people who receive these 6,159 secrets in this huge 955 page PDF document will want to obtain some of our other books and audio programs and participate in our special COACHING PROGRAMS. However, you are NOT obligated to buy anything—now or ever.

I know you're serious about making more money or you wouldn't be reading this. So go to: www.6159FreeSecrets.com and get this complete collection of 6,159 of my greatest marketing and success secrets right now! **You'll get this GREAT FREE GIFT in the next few minutes, just for letting me add you to my Client mailing list,** and I'll stay in CLOSE TOUCH with you... and do all I can to help you make even more money with my proven marketing strategies and methods.

So with all this said, let's begin...

** WARNING: This complete collection of 6,159 marketing and success secrets contains MANY CONTROVERSIAL ideas and methods. Also, it was originally written for MY EYES ONLY and for a few VERY CLOSE FRIENDS. Therefore, the language is X-RATED in some places [I got VERY EXCITED when I wrote many of these ideas and used VERY FOUL LANGUAGE to get my ideas across!] so 'IF' you are EASILY OFFENDED or do NOT want to read anything OFFENSIVE, then please do both of us a favor and DO NOT go to my website and download this FREE gift. THANK YOU for your understanding.

CHAPTER ONE

The secret to making <u>more</u> <u>money</u> in your business can be summed up in two words:

☞ THINK BIGGER! ☜

- ✓ You gotta keep your eye on the multi-million dollar (or billion!) prize!

- ✓ You <u>must</u> be willing to walk over a lot of $100.00 bills to get to the millions or billions you want.

- ✓ In other words, it's a fight for FOCUS! You must constantly put all of your time, attention, energy, and resources on the areas that can make you the most money.

Think Bigger!

The secret to making more money in any business can be summed up in just two words: think bigger! **You've got to keep your eye on the multimillion-dollar prize.** You've got to be willing to walk over a lot of hundred dollar bills in order to get the millions you want. In fact, if you're really thinking big, you don't want to make millions anymore; you're going for *billions* of dollars. **You've got to fight for focus and constantly put all your energy, time, attention, and resources into the areas that make you the most money.**

It requires no more effort or brainpower to think bigger. You don't actually have to pull the trigger on anything; just think bigger, that's all! **Try to establish a bigger vision for whatever it is you want to do.** Ask yourself some tough questions about what you're trying to accomplish—and don't just ask them once. Keep asking them over and over again! Ask yourself things like, "What's really possible for me? How high is my highest? What am I *really* capable of? In a perfect world, if I could have anything I really wanted, what would it be?" There are plenty of other questions you could come up with, but **be sure to ask yourself this one: "What do I want more than anything else—and why?"**

You've got to spend quality time dreaming big, thinking big, and even praying big. You can always be, do, and have more than you think. **In short, you're capable of more than you're demonstrating!**

Now, most people are terrified to think bigger, and focus way too much on the obstacles rather than the outcome. They agonize over all the things that might go wrong, rather than thinking about all the things that might go *right*. In doing so, they believe they're being smart. And sure, thorough contingency planning makes practical sense… but not in the very beginning. **Because what they're really doing by dwelling on those potential problems is limiting themselves. To think big, you have to let go of all your limitations.** Just dream a little—it doesn't take any more work to dream than not to. Don't stop yourself before you start by worrying that you'll make all kinds of mistakes!

Admittedly, that there are wild and crazy entrepreneurial types who think themselves bigger all the way to bankruptcy court. That's because they don't have any checks and balances in their lives; they haven't surrounded themselves with trustworthy people who can help them achieve their goals within the boundaries of reality. Remember the story of the Emperor's New Clothes? The Emperor is walking around naked, and the whole community is afraid to tell him he's making a fool of himself… until one little kid is brave (or innocent) enough to point out the Emperor's nudity. **I think there are some wild entrepreneurs out there who are just blowing up their companies, because their advisors are letting them get away with ideas that are far too grandiose or unrealistic.** They're thinking way *too* big, and don't know what the hell they're doing because they've surrounded themselves with "yes" people.

But for every entrepreneur who overdoes it, I **believe that there are *thousands* who never live up to their fullest potential, because they're afraid to "think outside the box."** Ultimately, the fear of overreaching themselves becomes terribly damaging and limiting.

When I was 24 years old, I read a book that changed my life: *The Magic of Thinking Big,* by David J. Swartz. It was the right book at the right time in my life, and I didn't just read that book; I devoured it. I read it and re-read it, mentally absorbing his teachings. I took it into my heart and head, because it's such a wonderful book. It was written in 1959, the year of my birth, and yet it's timeless. I just gave a copy to a would-be entrepreneur a few days ago, and I certainly hope that he reads it. In fact, I've given away hundreds of copies over the years, because I believe in Swartz's message so strongly; and I would encourage you to get that book as well. **The power in thinking bigger is crucial to business success, because it lets you access parts of yourself that you'd never have full access to otherwise.**

Everybody wants their income to expand, but they don't realize that the thinking comes first! **First you start thinking bigger, and *then* larger amounts of money come to you, because of the ideas you get when you think big.** Knowing what you're trying to do and why is so much more important than *how* you're trying to do it. So again, question yourself. Determine what you really want and how you need to get there. Every time you face a situation, ask yourself, "In a perfect world, if I could have anything that I really wanted here, what would it be?" **The answers you'll come up with will be amazing; sometimes,**

you'll actually surprise yourself. And those answers are within you right now! But you're locking yourself out of those potential possibilities if you're thinking too small, or focusing on all the things that might go wrong, instead of focusing on the big picture and actively trying to move towards it.

Back in the mid-1990s, a business associate of ours had a very successful product and a complete sales letter to sell that product with. He'd already generated huge sums of money with it. We tried to broker a joint venture deal with him, where we would mail his sales material to our customers and then split the profits; but all he wanted was a straight payment of $100,000 whereupon he would give us his sales material and the complete rights to duplicate that product at our own cost and sell it ourselves for 100% of the profits. **I could tell the profits would be phenomenal, because the costs to reproduce it were rock-bottom low, and the perceived value was sky-high. I knew that this would sell to our customers, so I took advantage of the offer and immediately wrote him a check.**

All our friends thought I'd lost my mind—that I'd become one of those reckless entrepreneurs with more money than brains. **But I knew what I was doing. We quickly turned that $100,000 into a million dollars, and went on to make a lot more money with it.** Even when that promotion tapped out, we were able to readapt that sales material for new products and services, and kept grafting off it to create new sales letters.

You see, we were thinking big, and had a specific plan in mind. It was a very simple plan; because a lot of times when you're thinking big, you're seeing it simple. That's part of the whole art of thinking this way. We had the last laugh on that one, because we made a lot of money in a hurry; **we were focused on the outcome, not the obstacles.** And of course, the biggest obstacle in this case would be, "Oh, my God, you're paying way too much for that!"

When I think of big thinkers, so many different entrepreneurs come to mind; but one of my favorites is Ted Turner. I've read a couple of bios on the man, and there's no doubt he's a big thinker, way ahead of his time. Turner's constantly thinking big. He took over his father's billboard business after the man committed suicide when Ted was 24. Ted Turner's father left him a business that was filled with problems, which is one of the reasons why he killed himself; that was the only solution he could find to alleviate his troubles. But again, Ted was a big thinker. **He fixed the business problems his father left him and, by thinking bigger than his father, he turned that business around.** Eventually Ted started buying TV stations... and we all know how that story ends.

Back in the late 1970s, he started developing the idea that would become CNN—the famous Cable News Network. There were many critics railing at him at the time, just coming out of the woodwork and telling him how he was doomed to fail. They ridiculed CNN as "The Chicken Noodle Network," predicting that Ted was going to lose all his money... and he almost did while getting it off the ground. It just barely putted along for quite a while, because he'd tried to bite off far more than he could chew. But through it all, Ted Turner continued to think bigger than everybody else. **He surrounded himself with good people, he thought bigger, and he became a billionaire.**

THINK BIGGER!

And then there's Ray Kroc. When he met the McDonald brothers in 1954, his business had recently taken a nosedive. He was struggling financially, he was 52 years old (the same age as I am right now), and he was desperate. He had to do something, and so he struck a deal with the McDonald brothers—and then he had a vision for taking that thing coast-to-coast, and then worldwide. **That vision materialized into the McDonald's restaurant chain of today. It also helped him beat out all of the competitors.** As I've pointed out before, about the time he got started—especially in the 1960's—there were literally hundreds of fast food chains. Some were rather small, but then McDonald's had started small; they all wanted to emulate what McDonald's and a couple of others were doing. But they couldn't, because they simply lacked his vision.

Now, that vision went beyond taking the whole thing nationwide. **It was also based on quality, innovation, and simply doing things right, along with a few other very strong concepts that Ray built his entire business philosophy around.** He also made sure he worked with the right groups of people to make his dream a reality.

Both Ted Turner and Ray Kroc were big thinkers, and that's something you see everywhere among the movers and shakers of the business world. If you study the biographies of self-made millionaires and billionaires, you'll see that they just thought bigger. I know it sounds simple, and it is. There's more to it than that, of course; but treat that as your entire operating system, and it'll be like you've replaced your old UNIVAC with a modern laptop computer. **Thinking bigger opens up all your filters, lets you tap into your fullest potential, and helps you**

do amazing things. And it's exciting! **Big thinkers energize those around them.** Nobody gets excited about small ideas; you can't cost-cut your way to prosperity. Big, bold things matter. **They get your staff excited, and more importantly, they get your *customers* excited, and cause them to flock to you.**

When I consider all the things that have been discovered and invented just in my lifetime, I can't help but be amazed. Consider personal computers, which first appeared in the 1980s and didn't really become hugely popular until the 1990s. Chris Lakey tells me that his family got their first computer when he was in 7th grade or 8th grade; his dad got it for work, and Chris was just enamored with the thing. It took up a whole desk and was pretty large, and the monitor was certainly big and clunky. He says it may even have been one of those monochrome ones... which I can tell you from personal experience were still in use well into the 1990s! Now, look at where the computer has come just since Chris was in junior high—not even 25 years ago! **Computers are getting smaller and smaller, because of the innovation driven by big thinkers who decided that they *should* be smaller, and ultimately that they should fit in the palm of your hand.**

And look at phones. These days, some are more powerful than that computer that took up a whole desk back when Chris was in junior high. **People in the telephony industry refused to accept things as they were; they thought there was a better way, and would stop at nothing to discover newer and better technologies to keep driving innovation forward.** As we're recording this, multiple versions of the iPhone have come out, and some people wonder why. Why did we even need iPhone2? Why wasn't the first iPhone good enough? Well, it's because someone thought big; because Steve Jobs said that the iPhone needed to be better. And they *have* gotten better as other technologies have come along.

Think about all the innovation you would have missed if everyone had just said, "Well, why do we need this?" Or, "Why can't we just accept things the way they are?" **All because people weren't able to think bigger. And it goes beyond modern electronics, because these things build on each other.** Go back 100 years; if the light bulb hadn't been invented, would we have had vacuum tubes for early radios and computers? The development of those things led to the technologies that we have today. Of course, if Edison hadn't invented the light bulb, someone else certainly would have. But imagine... before Edison *did* invent it, the idea that you could take a glass and wire, add some energy, and light up a whole room was pretty crazy thinking! We take it for granted now, but before the light bulb, that was thinking big!

These kinds of inventions and innovations, which changed lives and made things so much better for us today, weren't accidents. **They weren't caused by small thinkers.** The small thinkers are the ones who keep saying, "Well... the way we have it now is okay. There's no need to move beyond our sphere of accepted normalcy." **Big thinkers aren't content with the status quo.** Inventors like Edison dreamed bigger, and through the innovations that resulted, they gave us many of the things we take for granted these days and, in some cases, consider essential to civilized life. Did some of those big thinkers fail sometimes? Absolutely! **Some of them had multiple failures before finally**

succeeding. But the things they accomplished wouldn't have happened had they not been intent on big thinking, on imagining things above and beyond what was normally accepted.

Unfortunately, I think we've hit a point in our society where people have accepted mediocrity. Recently I read a newspaper article in our city paper about a school district handing out awards for attendance. These kids hadn't done anything except show up for school, and they were getting awards. Some people wrote in to say that this was good for the kids—that it helped them feel good about themselves, so self-esteem was higher, and it kept up the kids' morale. Other people wrote in saying how sad it is that we've accepted the idea that we should give awards for mediocrity. At a bare minimum, showing up for school is something required, and yet we're giving kids awards for accomplishing this?

Back when he was in school, Chris Lakey was in the school band. The music teacher always said at the beginning of the school year, **"There's a grade scale, and it starts at 'A' and ends in 'F.' Today, everybody is average.** Everybody starts out with a 'C'—and I'm going to assume that you're average unless you prove otherwise. So basically one of two things will happen over the course of this year: you'll practice like you're supposed to and you'll perform well, and that grade will go from average to a 'B' and hopefully an 'A.' On the flipside, if you're terrible and don't even do the bare minimum that you're supposed to do, you could go down from a 'C' to a 'D', or an 'F.'"

So just getting by, just being average, was going to result in a "C" for the class. Chris says that's where he fell most years.

THINK BIGGER!

He didn't want to fail, but he didn't want to achieve big things in band, either; so he did just enough to get by. Some of the kids excelled; and who knows, maybe they're making millions in rock bands these days!

The point is that average is just average. If you want to do bigger things, you have to think bigger than average, and you have to go beyond the normal. You see this throughout cultures, throughout history. There are certain people whom we look up to and say, "Wow, these are the big thinkers... these are the big dreamers," and you see the results of that action. It used to be that you wouldn't imagine anybody but NASA sending people into space—and now you've got private businesses trying to develop profitable space ventures. They talk about helping people go into space for tourism, for example. These things are possible (at least potentially) because someone thought bigger and they had the resources to support their dreams.

Similarly, the first people who thought that they could fly solo around the world (whether in airplanes or balloons) dreamed bigger than anyone had dreamed before. A few people dreamed that they could start companies that did things on the Internet that no one had ever imagined before. **In all these cases, you saw huge innovation as the people involved took their thinking beyond the normal—beyond what most people would accept.**

Sadly, this concept of normality, of how things are good enough as they are, tends to breed an attitude of complacency and mediocrity. You see this all around you in the people who tell you that you *shouldn't* dream big—folks who laugh at you when you say you want to have your own successful business. These people can't imagine you doing anything above and beyond what you're doing right now—or at least, that's what they *say*. People are always down on new ideas, especially big ones! **They're always telling you that you *can't*—even though there's no reason to think that you can't do something just because it's never been done before.** What happens is that we usually end up talking ourselves out of our dreams, because people have told us that we can't or shouldn't do that, or we shouldn't even try. After all, it's more than likely to fail, so you shouldn't even invest the effort. And a lot of times, those people end up being right about you failing; and it makes them feel and look good because they told you so. Even if you do succeed, those people rarely come back and tell you later, "I shouldn't have doubted you. You really pulled that one off!"

There are a lot of "Debbie Downers" out there, as some call them—people who tell you that you can't do something. Instead of surrounding yourself with them, **surround yourself with people who will encourage you to dream bigger, to think bigger, and to do whatever it takes to pull off those big dreams.** And it's not just enough to have those dreams. You've got to focus on the mission at hand and figure out what it takes to achieve those dreams and goals. Usually, it doesn't happen overnight; it requires a lot of hard work and dedication, some failure, and multiple outcomes along the way. **But if you aim for the stars, then you might hit the treetops; in fact, you might hit somewhere in between the trees and the stars.** But you certainly aren't going to hit the stars if you aim for the treetops... or the ground. You've got to have that goal out there, drawing you on.

THINK BIGGER!

Think bigger. Continuously push yourself beyond comfort level, beyond the point where you're prone to complacency. If you accept where you are today, there's probably not much left to help you push to where you want to be tomorrow. **You've got to always be out there on the forefront of what you feel is comfortable or doable.** The best way to get there is to believe that you *can* do it—to believe that it's possible, and then lay out the course of action you need to make it a reality. Always dream beyond what seems imaginable, but do everything you can to believe in those dreams. If your dreams are unbelievable to even you, you'll be less likely to try to make them happen. **So you do want realistic dreams—but always think bigger, and hopefully you'll hit the jackpot!**

The world is full of petty thinkers and critics, and here's part of the reason: they want to play it safe all the time. Another part of the reason is that critics are often right, while the big thinkers are wrong—and critics love to be right. But the truth is that a large percentage of new ideas fail, and so if all someone is doing is just sitting around and saying, "Oh, that won't work, that won't work, that won't work..." well, they're going to be right more often than not. They take such great superiority in trying to realize how much better they are than everybody else, because they're able to figure out all these things that are *not* going to work. **But that's simply no way to live. If you want more, you have to think bigger!**

During one of my early MLM experiences, I had a sponsor named Ron McFadden, and he was a former preacher. Boy, he really knew how to get a crowd rolling! I watched him in a couple of different situations where there were hundreds of people in the room, and Ron was center stage. One time he had us all chanting, "If you always think the way you've always thought, you're always going to get what you've always got." We just kept chanting that over and over again, working ourselves into a frenzy as they do at so many of these pep rallies. But it's true! *If you always think the way you've always thought, you're always going to get what you've always got.* You've got to expand your thinking to really succeed; you've got to be willing to take some huge risks and set some outrageous goals.

I think that, to a large degree, we've lost our way when it comes to thinking big. **Today, we don't have the same level of innovation and creativity that we had in decades past. That's to our detriment—and future generations will suffer, too, if we keep it up.** *There's no excuse for not thinking big.* Now, it's not a substitute for trying to examine all the possible things that can go wrong and having an answer for those things, too. But that comes later. **In the beginning, the goal has to be central to the whole thing; you can start picking it all apart later.** Thinking big from the word "go" is a much more exciting way to live! It's what separates those who achieve substantial and worthwhile things from everyone else... and it's something that anyone can do.

The cool thing here is that somebody who isn't blessed with a high IQ will always get further by thinking big than somebody who *does* have a high IQ and spends their whole life bogged down in the pettiness of small thinking, and always playing it safe.

CHAPTER TWO

The heart rules the mind!
(That's why we must sell to their emotions!)

Sell to the Prospect's Emotions

The heart rules the mind, and that's why we must always sell to the prospect's emotions. **People tend to buy for emotional rather than for logical reasons, and the two biggest motivating emotions are always (and will always be) greed and fear, or some combination thereof.** There are other important emotions too, of course, like love, guilt, and pride; but greed and fear are the two ruling forces that are always with us, controlling our actions from the cradle to the grave.

That being the case, you have to give those emotions serious consideration, to the point where you get well beyond a superficial understanding of your prospects, **digging deep into the true factors that motivate people to buy.** What are their biggest hopes, fears, and desires? What are they *really* searching for? What are their biggest failures and frustrations? What gets them excited the most, and why? Those are the kinds of questions you need to ask yourself.

Your job is to get behind their eyeballs—get inside their heads and hearts—so you can decode these unconscious motivators. These aren't things that our customers and prospects can easily articulate, because emotions are basically subconscious; that is, people aren't in tune with their emotions most of the time. **So the more you think about and identify with the people you want to reach in your marketplace, the**

more you'll understand them and the behavior that makes them buy. Knowing what you know about their psychology, you may even come to understand them better than they understand themselves, at least on this point.

It's your job to delve in their minds just like a good psychologist would do. In fact, one of the best definitions of marketing that I've ever been taught (and taught others) is that marketing is just a combination of psychology and math. **Your job, like the psychologist's, is to understand the reasons for the prospect's behavior, if only in this very narrow sense.** Leave the rest of their emotional lives to the shrinks; we're only concerned about them from a buying perspective. That facet of their psychology is absolutely vital for you to understand.

I think it's also vital for you to try to understand why *you* buy the things you do. Why are *you* compelled to spend money? The next time you feel the need to spend money on something, stop yourself at some point in the process and ask yourself *why* you're doing it. I think you'll find that you're being controlled by your emotions to some extent. There may be logical justifications for the purchase, but consider this: **are you really just buying what you want to buy, and adding the justifications after the fact?** I'll bet it's the latter. You get caught up in your emotions, and buy want you want or need.

Emotions fuel all kinds of behavior, and the best examples are always the most extreme. So let's look at other things that people do for purely emotional reasons. How about gambling? I used to have something of a gambling problem. Every time I got around a casino, I just lost control. I'd spend all my money and then borrow more from my wife and friends—and spend all that, ending up disappointed and bummed out. Overall, I'd have a miserable experience. Well, the last time I was in Vegas for a seminar, I told myself, "I am not going to spend one single dollar on gambling. I will not! I won't even put a single token into a slot machine. I won't do it!"

I was just so tired of being controlled by my emotions and having bad experiences. I kept my promise to myself, and avoided gambling for the entire three days I was there. And because I wasn't caught up in the heat of my emotional behavior, I was able to see all kinds of interesting things I'd never seen before. **My whole perspective had changed. I was able to be very objective about many things that had to do with gambling.** I walked through the casinos, I watched the other gamblers, I saw myself in their behavior, and it was truly an enlightening experience.

I've had the same problems with purchasing products at marketing seminars in the past. Often, I'd end up spending thousands of dollars on products that I would never actually use. I'd get caught up in the day-to-day aspects of the business after I got home, I'd let the products I'd bought go to waste, and then I would always feel terrible about myself. **I knew I was out of control with my buying; but the emotions would just take over, as they often do.** Well, the last time I went to a marketing seminar I promised myself—just as I had with gambling on that Vegas trip—that I wasn't going to spend any money there. I'd already spent several thousand dollars just to get to the seminar, but I wasn't going to buy anything they were selling.

And again, because I wasn't busy buying, I was able to see things I hadn't before. I was able to watch closely all of those presenters up on stage as they performed their sales magic—the same sales magic that normally worked on me. **This time, I was able to achieve a level of objectivity that helped me perceive the tricks behind their sales presentations—and I learned a whole lot.** It was fascinating just watching these guys perform, learning how they crafted and structured their offers, identifying the emotional hot buttons they were going after and the various techniques they were using to sell the crowd. **It was quite educational—a wonderful refresher course on selling, which I was able to enjoy and prosper from because I wasn't allowing myself to be sold.**

So catch yourself the next time you're in the heat of buying something. **Pull back and actually force yourself not to buy. Try to understand the behavior that got you there—because this is the key to understanding the buying behavior of other people.** It's the true secret to understanding why other people do what they do; and you have to be able to understand it in yourself, because for everyone else, it's unconscious behavior. The same is true for you until you decide you're going to make it conscious. So think about that. When you pull back and tell yourself you're not going to buy whatever it is you're so crazy about, you can achieve that level of objectivity that I had at my last marketing seminar. You'll see new things. You'll learn new things. **You'll do what I call "getting on the other side of the cash register."**

Instead of thinking like a consumer or a buyer, you'll start thinking like a seller. You can never really learn to put yourself in the prospect's shoes if you're caught up in the emotion of it yourself. **If you're always a customer, you're never going to learn how to *sell* to that customer.** You're going to be too close to the forest to see the individual trees. By pulling back and forcing yourself not to buy things (except our products, of course!) then you'll start to see the tricks behind the magic.

So what are those tricks? **First of all, we use lots of stories to sell: before-and-after stories, comparison stories, stories to build value in what we're offering, stories to compare what we have with something else of much greater value, stories to help get us below the radar screen of the average prospect.** Because, remember: while most prospective buyers do get caught up in their emotions—and we need them to, because the emotions drive the sale—**they're also very skeptical.** They've got their guard up to some degree, more so today than ever before. **Good stories get you past that guard.** While people hate to be sold, everybody loves a good story—especially if it's told well.

The better you are at telling stories, the more likely you'll evade the prospect's radar screen. **A good story triggers their emotions without them realizing it.** It helps you establish the value for what you're selling, it helps them understand what you're trying to get across to them, and it helps them see themselves in the picture, especially that happy "after" picture of the before-and-after story. **Every time you hear marketers tell stories, or read the stories they write, that's what they're trying to do: evade your guard, fly under your radar, or otherwise get past your natural skepticism.**

And when I say "stories," I also mean analogies, metaphors, and anecdotes as well; that is, various ways of comparing things to other things. **These stories make you and your products less threatening to people, which means they're more likely to spend their money with you.** Realize that your prospects are always trying *not* to spend money, at least to some degree. As a result, you'll face some real resistance—so you've got to do things to get them excited. The more excited somebody is, the more their emotions are going to carry them away! So, what can you do to really make them excited? Well, in many ways, **selling is a transference of the emotions... so you have to be excited yourself. Get yourself all worked up.** The more you believe in the value of what you're selling—the more you believe that it really can give your buyers what they're looking for—the more you can convince them of that. **People have to be able to see themselves enjoying the benefits. Enthusiasm sells, so catch yourself on fire!**

But don't overdo it. Sell the sizzle, not the steak. **So many people ruin the sale by revealing all the details right away, instead of trying to get people super-excited first.** So what can you do to make people more excited about what you're selling? What can you do to make your offer more desirable? Here's an idea: **why not give away something valuable?** At the moment, we're in the process of creating some huge campaigns where we're giving away items of extreme value as premiums to drive the sale. These are items that people really want, and we play them up in a big way. That gets the prospects excited about the free premium. **Of course, getting the premium is conditional on making the purchase; but their desire for it often pushes them over the edge. FREE is something that goes right to the**

greed glands!

So think about how you can apply premiums to your own offers. Pay more attention to what other people are doing, especially those who are making the most money. They're not making all that money by accident. They've learned how to master the art of tapping into emotions—and it *is* an art form, rather than a science. There's not a formula to follow, though there are certain things that you can point to, and I've mentioned some of them here. **The people who are best at it have elevated it to the point where they make it look natural; you don't even know that you're being sold.** So watch them and learn. Try to pull back and stay objective; get on the other side of that cash register, and use their methods as a model. The same kinds of things that are making millions of dollars for others can do the same for you.

In addition to the basic psychology of the system, step back and look at economics in general. I think that's a great way to start understanding the psychology of purchasing, since no matter how big it may be in a macroeconomic sense, an economy is made up of all of the little transactions that occur as people buy and sell things. And the truth is, an economy isn't a monolithic thing. **We don't have one economy; we have a million little ones that add together on a wider scale.** For example, we have the economy of our company, and the amount of business we do with our clients. McDonald's has their economy, which is made up of all those cheeseburgers and French fries that they sell. Wal-Mart has the Wal-Mart economy; and all these individual economies fall into groups—the wider business opportunities economy, the fast food economy, the mercantile economy. **All those transactions, dollar by dollar, add up to the nationwide and worldwide Economy.**

All economies, then, are made up of the accumulation of small transactions. When you look closely at those small transactions, you really start seeing where, as a society, we spend our money. **You learn things about the people making those individual transactions, based on their buying habits.** Beyond a certain governmental level, you can't easily control what people buy in a free market, so their spending habits can't help but be somewhat revealing.

People in a free market will choose to buy what they want to buy. They choose whether they're going to go to McDonald's or Burger King, or to a place that just serves salads. They choose what kind of socks to wear. They make the determination on whether they should buy a fuel-efficient hybrid car or a gas-guzzler, or whether they're going to purchase an Apple or a Microsoft computer. Those decisions, which all affect our larger economy a tiny bit, are based on emotions. **Remember: the heart rules the mind.** When it comes to selling, you have to understand this basic economic principle — because contrary to what our government likes to think, you can't steer an economy using rational thought.

Suppose you were to ask people, "Does it make sense to spend $100 a week for the gasoline necessary to run a big V-8 engine, when you could drive a sub-compact electric vehicle for a small fraction of that price?" Most folks would agree in principle that it *doesn't* make sense from an economic standpoint. But most people don't really care about being economical. **People don't always make decisions based on what's in their best interests; some commentators might say they *never* do. People tend to buy for emotional reasons.**

Now, admittedly, in some cases people do have practical buying reasons that are mixed up with their emotional reasons; for example, someone might buy a pickup truck because they're thinking, "A little sub-compact just won't be able to tow my camping trailer." In this case, there are practical reasons why you would want Option A over Option B. But let's consider a Corvette. No one *really* needs a Corvette for practical purposes; you buy a Corvette for emotional reasons. For example, maybe you're a middle-aged man going through a mid-life crisis, and you feel like a 'Vette will impress the ladies. Maybe you simply like the way you feel while driving a fast, fancy sports car.

Clearly, there's no practical reason to own a Corvette. No one could honestly say, "I bought this car for practical reasons. This was purely an economic decision; it was simply the best use of my money." And yet Corvettes are among the most popular sports cars around. I think they illustrate perfectly the fact that many purchases are based on emotional logic, if there's any "logic" there at all. **When you can look at that fact and accept it, then the decisions you make on how to reach your marketplace come from the proper mindset.** You can more easily identify which emotions are affecting your prospects, what they would be inclined to respond to, and what triggers would make them want to do business with you. **Of course, all that depends on the marketplace you're in, who your prospects are, and the benefits they're looking for.** That's knowledge you'd better have down cold.

Again, all this can be hard to implement when you're exposed to the marketing yourself, because you also tend to succumb to the emotions of buying, even if you try not to. It's one reason that some people put "No Soliciting" signs on their doors. They know that if you come and solicit, they're likely to buy because they can't help themselves—so they'd rather you not come at all. **But if you can put aside the consumer mentality for a while, so that you can look at the things that are making people want to buy, you'll be able to develop a better idea of what it takes to sell to your prospects.**

Become a cautious customer in your marketplace, if you're not already, and look at the way that buying and selling takes place within that marketplace. **See what other marketers are doing, see how they sell, and examine the emotional triggers that other people are responding to.** Take notes, and spend some time processing the emotional response to the advertising. **Then develop your own strategies for using emotions to sell, paying close attention to the details of why folks in your marketplace respond as they do.**

And don't feel bad doing all this. Some people feel that by applying this strategy, you're using people's emotions against them. But realize that the people in your marketplace didn't come to you *without* these emotions. They already had them, and in most cases, they've already bought something from somebody else using those very same emotions. **This is simply the reality of human nature and behavior; and in as much as you can use that as a tool to help you understand your**

marketplace and then sell to your prospects, you're going to be better positioned to dominate.

Now, that doesn't mean that you shouldn't back up your offer with the facts; of course you should, because **people do want to feel like they're making good decisions.** Even if they're buying based on emotions, they want it backed up with logic. But just keep in mind that most people are buying based not on the facts and figures, but on the emotions behind the decision.

Look at what good politicians and religious leaders do. Look at the way they attract people's attention and reel them in. They're great communicators. They know how to get you pumped up. **They tell lots of stories, and use plenty of analogies and colorful metaphors.** There's a reason for this. **It's good communication, but it also hooks you in emotionally, pulling you into their world—and that's exactly what you need to do with all your own marketing.**

If you get nothing else out of this discussion, **remember that you need to focus on telling more stories to draw people in emotionally, and help drive your sales points home.**

CHAPTER THREE

In any negotiation...

The person who pretends like they need or want it <u>the</u> <u>least</u> — WINS!

Pretend You Want It the Least

All selling is negotiation. You're trying to get their money; they're trying to keep it. **Well, here's another fact of life to remember: in any negotiation, the person who pretends they want the outcome the least is almost always the one who wins.** If you'll adapt that as one of your strategies, you're likely to close more deals.

Now think about that: it's just a big acting game, isn't it? **If you've got a hot prospect, they'll try not to show you just how excited they are, because they sense that to do so puts them at a disadvantage.** They're right. And, of course, it's the same with you as the marketer or the salesperson; **you don't want to appear too eager to make the sale.** You've got to see it as a game. **Whoever wants it the least wins... or at least, whoever *pretends* they want it the least wins.**

There's an old quote that I memorized years ago from the world of dating, well before I was ever in business, that goes, "You've got to run until they catch you." So how does it apply to business? **In a nutshell, people love to buy things… but they hate to be *sold* anything.**

You might ask, "What's the difference?" **Basically, when people buy something without being pressured, they feel that they're the ones doing the choosing—the chasing, if you will.**

THINK BIGGER!

People like to chase after things, but they don't necessarily like being chased. The minute they start feeling chased, they start backing up. Your goal as a marketer must be to put your prospects at ease, and make them feel as if they're the ones chasing after you rather than vice-versa.

This is one of the biggest reasons why two-step marketing is our primary marketing vehicle here at M.O.R.E., Inc. In Step #1, we offer people something for low cost or no cost. We make it very easy for them to take that first step; and when they do, their perception changes. **Do this right, and you can put the psychological advantage on your side of the court—because once people raise their hands in Step #1, they begin to feel that they're the ones who came to you.** They forget that it was your magazine ad or direct mail package that started them on this path. All they know is, they've chosen to respond to your offer, which makes them feel empowered— and that's really what people want. They don't want to feel they're being taken advantage of, or that you're coming on to them too strong. They want to be in control, so you've got to make them feel as if they are... even as you arrange things so that in reality, *you're* the one in control.

And yes, it *is* kind of manipulative. But then again, all selling is. There was a book out years ago called *Non-Manipulative Selling*; that's a big fat joke! There's *no such thing* as non-manipulative selling. You're trying to get people to give you their money; they're trying to keep hold of their money as long as they can, while trying to get the best deal they can. **It's an inherently manipulative process. But that's fine when you're trading value for value:** when you have something that truly delivers on your promises, when your product or service really does for them everything that you say it can do. **That's how you sleep peacefully at night, because you know you're delivering something valid.**

Now, in the dating world (as I vaguely recall from the days when I was single), most guys do a terrible job of "running until they catch you," as I suggested earlier; though there are notable exceptions. Guys are usually the ones doing the chasing, right? Women are much better at applying this principle. Back in the day, I'd often see women with two or three guys on the string. The girl would play hard to get, increasing her attractiveness in the eyes of the men chasing her—and that's what you have to do in business, too. **You have to act like the prospect needs you a lot more than you need them. That means you can never let yourself seem too eager to get their business.** You have to pull back a little, and sometimes you have to do things like position yourself an expert—something I'll discuss in more detail later.

One thing you should definitely do is create strong cut-off dates for your offers, and stick to them. We've all seen businesses that advertise "Going Out of Business" sales that last for years. After a while, you stop believing them, and the urgency's gone. So you have to tell people, "Look, you have until this date and then it's over," and then stop selling when that date comes. **This often tips the balance, forcing them to act while they still can.** Again, they feel they're the ones doing the choosing—but they forget that you're the one who set that deadline.

We have a sale every December here at M.O.R.E., Inc.

It ends on December 31. When the clock strikes midnight and the calendar rolls over to January 1, that's it: the offer is off the table. We start promoting in November, and build the whole campaign around that strict deadline. **We use lots of follow-up marketing containing plenty of repetition, so it gets stuck in people's heads.** But the truth is, very seldom will people actually wonder, "Huh, I wonder if the deal's still going to be available to me on January 10?" We're the ones who establish the whole thing, but people buy into it, and they forget that we put the idea in their heads. All they know is, "Man, I've got to hurry up and respond because this is over at midnight December 31," never once realizing that, for all they know, they could still get the same offer on January 2. They can't, but we make sure they don't even entertain the possibility.

It's all about positioning yourself as the one in power. **Selling is negotiation; don't let anybody tell you any different.** You need to negotiate from a strong position, which means you must be credible. This is where your expert status becomes important. The more you can do to position yourself as an expert, the more money you can make. You're utilizing some powerful psychological tools here, because authority is one of the six factors of human influence. **The more you become an expert at something, the more you represent authority.**

At the time of this writing, we have six client service representatives here at M.O.R.E., Inc. The problem is that our average prospects see our customer service reps as mere salespeople. We haven't positioned them otherwise... because after all, show me any expert who's going to cold call somebody. Salespeople do it every day, but an expert? A real authority on something? No way are they going to call you out of the blue. **They've going to have somebody do the buildup for you.** They're going to have a secretary, at least, who calls you first and sets an appointment. If you don't make the appointment, that same secretary is going to get on the phone and chew you out.

That's one aspect of this sort of positioning. You don't stand your lawyer or your accountant up. **If you've got an appointment with a professional, you're probably going to keep it.** But we walk over salespeople all day long. We hang up on them, we abuse them; we say things and do things to salespeople that we wouldn't think about doing to anybody else. The reason we do it is because in our minds, they're nothing much; just salespeople.

To get past a roadblock like that, you have to establish yourself as an authority; and to do that, you have to spend some money—which is one of the reasons most companies don't do anything substantial on this front. Well, we're going to push the boundaries. We're going to test this idea. We're not going to be aggressive with it, but we're going to slowly work up and develop the positioning around our client service representatives so they're elevated in the eyes of our prospective buyers. **They're not just salespeople, and we want our prospects to realize that.** Each of them is going to have a secretary. Of course, three salespeople might share the same secretary… but our customers don't need to know that!

In any case, their secretary will call and set the stage with the prospect; so that when the customer service rep gets them on the telephone, the rep won't just be somebody trying to sell the prospect something. **They'll be a consultant; they'll be an expert; they'll be a professional! This is one part of our strategy of letting them chase us, rather than us chasing them.**

Right now, all our salespeople are doing is chasing after people—and it's a rough way for them to make a living. Believe me, they're getting burned out on the whole process. **It's tough to be a salesman.** I know that firsthand; I spent years at it. I've had doors slammed in my face more times than I could ever want to remember. I've had thousands of people say "no" to me personally. I've had many people call me names and hang up on me on the phone. Ah, but if you're a professional, you have it easier. How often does your lawyer or doctor get hung up on or cussed out or have doors slammed in his face? I'm sure it does happen, but not that often.

Again, it's about positioning. It's about putting yourself in that position of power. **It's about *you* controlling the whole negotiation process, but making the prospect feel like *they're* controlling it.** There's an art to this. If you have no experience at it, then study how other people are doing it and emulate them. That's really what it all boils down to: **you need to make the prospect feel they're in power, while in actuality controlling that power yourself.** Otherwise, you just do whatever your prospects want, which is a less profitable position. If you can control that relationship but give the appearance of the prospect controlling it, it will benefit you greatly. If you lose control of that, so that it benefits the prospect entirely, they may not become a customer at all.

And make no mistake: this must be done under the assumption that the product or service you sell is of real value and benefit to your marketplace. For example, if I go into McDonald's and see that a Big Mac meal is going to set me back six bucks, I need to feel, at the very minimum, that the meal is worth that six bucks—that it's an even exchange. For McDonald's to really win, they need to make me to feel like it's a steal—like it's worth 20 bucks, so if I'm getting it for *six* bucks, it's a bargain. At some point we come to an agreement that my money is a good exchange for that Big Mac. The food ends up in my stomach, the money ends up in their cash register, and we both go about our business. **So ultimately, during any transaction, the buyer comes to a determination that the money is at least equal in value to the products or services they're receiving.** In some cases the seller feels like they won, and in some cases the consumer feels like *they* won. **In the best circumstances, they both feel like winners.**

And keep in mind that many buyers get pleasure from the entire purchasing experience. For example, Chris Lakey tells me he actually enjoys buying a car. It excites him to be in that mode where you're sitting down across the table from someone and staring them in the eyes, and you're passing papers back and forth as the numbers are written down, and you're negotiating a final purchase price. Maybe Chris just enjoys it because he's a marketer; I know that a lot of people hate that experience.

In any case, I think that the car-buying experience is a simple, easy-to-understand example of the balance-of-power equation in a business transaction. The art of negotiation takes place every day in car dealerships all over the U.S., and most likely the world; I assume it works the same way everywhere, though what I've experienced might be strictly a U.S. phenomenon. **In any case, once you've had the test drive and you sit down at the salesman's desk, that's when the negotiation begins in earnest.** You have to be very careful at this point. Perhaps you let it slip that you have no choice but to get a new car, and that you're desperate to do so. Perhaps you let it slip that you can afford a payment of $500 a month. Most likely, during the test drive you revealed a lot of information about yourself in casual conversation with the salesperson.

So let's say you get to the negotiation phase, and that salesman knows that you can afford to spend $500 a month, he knows that you really like the car (because you told him that while you were driving), he knows that you're desperate, and automatically, for some odd reason, the payment on this car you want is only $499.00 a month. It fits right in precisely with what you're looking for—and now you've lost any ability to negotiate, because you told them your negotiation points. **From this point, negotiations become difficult for you. You've already outlined all the perimeters for your coming to an agreement, so you have very little (if any) room left to maneuver.**

As a consumer, you want to reveal as little as possible to your salesperson. You don't want to tell them if you have a trade-in, for example, because immediately that becomes a factor in your ability to do business. You don't want to tell them about the $500 off coupon you printed off their website. The more you reveal to the salesperson, the more you put them at an advantage; so you want to negotiate the best price you can for that car outside of all these other factors. **The more you can keep things close to your chest, the less likely they are to get a deal that benefits them at your expense.** This puts you in the position of power, as opposed to the car salesman.

The truth is, in the scope of car buying there's really not a bad deal to be had, outside of someone selling you a lemon intentionally. But let's say the sticker price is $20,000. If you can negotiate a price that's a few thousand less than that, then usually both parties are happy. If you pay sticker price for it, you're just paying what they're asking. Some people might call you a "sucker," but still, there's no harm in that if you don't want to have to deal with negotiations. You can walk onto any lot today and buy just about any car that you can afford without haggling.

Whatever you do, in the end, buying a car is just two people coming together and agreeing on the terms of a price and conditions under which one will buy a car. Chris enjoys that whole process. In fact, he recently bought a car from a private individual, with whom he negotiated directly. Chris is happy and thinks that the other guy's happy, which is the best possible kind of transaction. Now, Chris knows that the car he bought might have some hidden things wrong with it. It's an older car, just for driving back and forth to work, and it did have a few minor things that needed to be fixed. He used that to his advantage, and negotiated the price lower than he would have otherwise. **So the person who was selling it provided information to Chris based on questions he asked that allowed him to feel like he won in the transaction, and in the end they made a deal.**

But all during the process, Chris visited a lot of dealerships, and made it a goal to tell salespeople, "I'm in no hurry to buy a car. I've got no issues with waiting." He made it clear that he was noncommittal. **By showing the salesmen that there was no rush, he put himself at an advantage over them,** because they knew that he had no problem walking away—that, in fact, he was much more likely to leave without a car than with one. If they didn't find a car that was perfect for him, well, he wasn't going to buy it. He wasn't just going to settle on anything; and he surely wasn't going to consider a different kind of car than the one he wanted. **His parameters were narrow, and that put the pressure on them, taking it off him.**

In that case Chris was the consumer, but the same thing applies if you're the seller. **If you pretend you need or want to make the sell less than the prospect wants to buy what you're offering, you're going to win more often than not.** There may be situations where that doesn't hold true; but I do know that if the customer feels you're desperate, then they're more likely to win in the game of salesmanship. You're less likely to make a profit, because you'll have to give up something to make that deal. If your price is $1,000 for your widget and someone feels you're desperately trying to make that sale, then all of a sudden you start having to add perks or benefits—or lowering the base price. You have to start "giving away the store," as they say. Or maybe they're bolder in asking for discounts. All of a sudden you're at a disadvantage, because they feel they have power in the relationship.

On the other hand, suppose you tell people, "Hey, this is the price. If you don't want it at this price, I've got other people lined up who do. I'm sorry if it doesn't work out for you, but we need to part ways quickly, because these folks are ready to make a decision." **Being blunt like this puts them at a disadvantage.** It puts them on alert that you don't really need their business; so if they're not going to make a purchase, would they kindly step aside so you can work with the next person in line?

This strategy puts you in control. They know that you have the advantage, and it's up to them to decide whether to play ball or not. And that's really what it's about in the art of negotiation. **Whoever gains control immediately usually wins. And again, this all occurs within the confines of a healthy negotiation and in a scenario where, ultimately, both parties feel like they've won.** There's no overt coercion. They don't have to play ball if they don't want to. The reality here is that one of you has to come out on top; and while you do want to deliver good value to the customer, in the end—as a salesperson or a business owner—you want that person on top to be you. And you want the customer to know that you were in control the whole time, even though they felt like they also had control… or at least, that they got a good deal out of it too.

Just remember that if people feel like they're running after you, they're more likely to pay you what you're asking for than if they feel like *you're* chasing *them*. It's a psychological quirk that's hard to understand, but it's nonetheless true that the more people feel like they're the ones doing the hunting, the more they feel like they're in control. As a result, they feel like there's less pressure for them to buy. **The triggers that make people put up sales resistance aren't tripped when they feel that they're the ones looking to do**

business with you. Otherwise, the shields go up.

You've experienced this, I imagine, whenever you get a sales call. I got a call like that the other day—and it was the craziest thing. You know the sound of a foghorn, like you hear from barge or a cruise ship? That real low hum was what I heard when I answered the phone—and then someone started telling me that they were giving me a cruise. I hung up on them before I could get any further; I just don't want to go on a cruise right now. I'm sure that this is a lovely company, and if I were looking to buy a cruise, then I would have been happy to talk to them. But they sought me out, I wasn't interested at that moment, and I hung up before I could even hear what their offer was. On the other side, if I *had* been looking for a cruise, I would have been seeking *them* out. I would have done everything I could to get as much information about that offer as possible. **So it all comes down to how you position your offer, how you position yourself, and the strategies you use.** Again, you want people to feel like *they're* in control in a buying situation, even when you hold the ultimate power.

And don't be afraid to say "no" to an offer or to a negotiation. Don't be afraid to say, "This isn't going to work out; let's part ways." Usually, what that means is that the prospects are more likely to want to chase you anyway. **If you tell them they can't have something, the first thing people want to do is get ahold of it. Use that to your advantage!**

As I mentioned earlier, when you use a two-step offer (as we often do here at M.O R.E., Inc.), **prospects get the feeling they're chasing after you, even though you approached them**

first. And there's one thing you'll always know about them: that they really *are* interested, because they qualified themselves by raising their hands in the first place. Maybe you got them to spend a little money on your introductory offer. Furthermore, when you know you have a qualified prospect, and you know that your product or service really does deliver on the goods, then you're doing those prospects a tremendous disservice if you don't do everything short of physical violence to get them to buy from you.

Let me tell you a quick story to demonstrate the potential for total power and control in the negotiation process. Most salespeople have heard that in a face-to-face or even in a telephone-selling environment, **once you do your presentation and complete your close, the person who speaks first is generally the one who loses**. Well, we have a sales rep here named Shannon Morris, and he's been selling for over a decade. At a seminar a few years ago, he had a prospective buyer in front of him. Shannon had delivered his presentation, answered all the guy's objections, and done his close. He put the contract in front of the customer and then just shut up, like every good salesperson is supposed to do.

The prospect was resisting, too. He didn't want to sign the whole deal; he was trying to hold onto his money. In other words, the prospect was trying to hold onto all the power... but so was Shannon. **For over 15 minutes (we timed him), Shannon just stood there, looking at the guy right in the eye.** The prospect stood there looking Shannon right in the eye in return, and neither one of them was going to budge. **Shannon stayed very calm. Fifteen minutes is an eternity in a**

negotiating situation. That takes nerves of steel.

For 15 minutes, the prospect didn't say anything to Shannon; for 15 minutes, Shannon didn't say anything to the prospect. They just stood there silently, face-to-face, for a full quarter-hour... and ultimately, Shannon got the sale! **The guy finally filled out the order form and gave it to Shannon.**

That's an extreme example, but think about it: who had the power in this situation? They were struggling for control of it, but ultimately, Shannon won. He wanted it the most, and that's what it's all comes down to. Shannon made his offer, he answered the prospect's objections, he put the contract in front of the prospect... and then he shut up, quietly waiting for the prospect to make his choice. **He just did his job and let the other guy make the decision, as if it didn't matter to him whether the guy signed or not.** He maintained control of the situation for as long as it took to make the sale—and he made sure that the prospect was the one who did the chasing.

Think deeply about how you can apply that concept to your own business.

CHAPTER FOUR

Let your communications buzz with excitement!

The <u>greatest sin of all</u> is to bore somebody!

Let Your Communications Buzz with Excitement!

When you're a marketer, the greatest sin of all is to bore somebody.

We all know people just put you to sleep, and that's fine on a personal level; it doesn't hurt anything. But you absolutely can't do that from a business and a marketing perspective. **You have to excite people! You have to be enthusiastic! You have to display passion!** So much of the marketing out there now has zero passion. There's no real enthusiasm to it, which perplexes me — because it's a truism that bored people don't buy. Only excited, enthusiastic people buy and keep on buying.

So: how do they get enthusiastic? By *you* getting enthusiastic! **Selling is a transference of emotion, so the more excited and passionate you are about what you're trying to sell, the more excited and passionate your prospects will be.** Remember, people buy for emotional reasons. That's why they do *everything* they do.

So you've got to be excited about every aspect of your marketing. First of all, you've got to find a market that excites you, and then find (or create) something you have true enthusiasm for. Don't just enter a market because of the moneymaking potential. Do it because you love it and can honestly get excited about it. **That love — that passion, that**

enthusiasm, that energy—will then be easy for you to share with other people. The last thing you want to do is try to fake your enthusiasm. Contrary to popular belief, most people can spot phonies instantly. **You need to have a genuine, natural enthusiasm for whatever you're doing, or you'll fail.**

Think about the best salespeople you've ever met. What qualities did they share? I'll bet what you remember most is their passion, enthusiasm, and excitement. Now, those aren't especially rare qualities; most of us can develop them for our true interests. Passion and enthusiasm can be a quiet thing, too. But when you apply it to marketing, however you decide to handle it, you've got to get people excited! **When you write a headline, it has to express your product's biggest, most exciting benefit.** All sales copy and advertising must be exciting and enthusiastic. **If it's flat, you won't make many sales.** There are too many marketing messages out there, so anything that doesn't immediately strike a chord with the prospect is going to get drowned. Whatever you do, let your communications buzz with excitement!

This principle works for just about anything in life. Let's take sports as an example, because it's something that many people are passionate about. Football is probably my favorite sport, and of course I'm a Kansas City Chiefs fan. Let's say it's a Monday morning after an exciting win, and the Chiefs come up in conversation. If I say, "Yep, they played yesterday. It was a good game," well, that's boring, isn't it? And frankly, that's usually the way the Chiefs have played in the past! After a loss, that's the way the conversation goes. But if they win, I'm supposed to be excited. **If I talk in a plain monotone and I'm**

just factual, I'm not exactly going to infect anyone with my enthusiasm and make them want to become a Chiefs fan. "Yeah, they played a game. It was good. They won, and I'm sure glad they outscored their opponent. Did you see that 55-yard field goal? Boy, he barely got that one across the goal line, didn't he? Rah rah rah."

Remember Eeyore, the donkey in Winnie The Pooh? He talks reeeaaalllyyy slowly, and he's always down on everything: "Woe is me." C'mon—no one really wants to be a part of that kind of conversation! So if you're talking sports, you're usually enthusiastic. You're fired up about your team, and even when your team's stinkin' it up, you're fired up about being mad about them stinking! **And so you speak with passion and conviction, with an urgent energy.** You get all jacked up and you're elevated in your conversational tone.

Chris Lakey likes talking politics, and he can get really energetic and passionate about the subject. **Well, when you're selling your product or service, you need to get as fired up as you might by sports or politics.** When you're enthusiastic about something, your heart rate is elevated, and your body language is different; everything goes up a notch. Your communication *buzzes* with excitement.

Chris and I were talking about the health market recently, and discussed how you feel when you experience relief from a long-term health problem. **You tend to be excited about it, and talk to people about it. That's a natural outflow of the experience that you've had at a personal level.** You've found a cure, and want to spread the good news. People who experience something like that tend to be enthusiastic as they share that news.

As a marketer, you have to transfer that face-to-face enthusiasm into other media. Here at M.O.R.E., Inc., we sell by mail, so most of our advertising is done using the printed word. We write a letter and mail that letter to a prospect. **In order to generate interest (and therefore, sales), that letter has to convey the buzz we're feeling about the product or the service we're offering.** If that letter feels like Eeyore talking, if that letter is empty of emotion and void of excitement, the person reading it isn't going to have any fun reading it. They're certainly not going to feel like we're passionate about our own product, and they're probably not going to be interested in buying it.

Let's say I'm trying to sell you a new smartphone. I could say something like, "Hey, the MyPhone 4 makes phone calls. You can check your email on it. You can browse the web. Oh, and it has a built-in camera, so you can take pictures." That might be factual, but it's boring. On the other hand, if I talk about how excited I am about this new device, that enthusiasm may very well rub off on the prospect. Suppose I say, "The MyPhone 4 will do all kinds of things! You can tell it to make appointments for you, and it will! You can tell it you want to text somebody, and it'll just do it! It'll probably even go to the bathroom for you if you really want it to! That's the next app! **I'm so excited about the MyPhone! Everybody should have a MyPhone!** Your boring old flip phone could never do anything like this! This phone will do *everything* for you!" That's how you generate excitement about a product.

In your sales copy, you have to do the same thing. **You want to transfer your buzz to the reader.** If you can get them excited, they're more likely to buy your product because you've conveyed your own enthusiasm, and you've gotten them into a position where they want to feel the results you've promised them. **The only way they can go to the next level is to buy your product or service, so they can feel that buzz directly.**

In my test ads for my book *The Miracle Cure*, which came out in November 2011, I'm using a story of a lady that I've known for about 30 years. Her name is Mary Jones; she's my graphic artist. **Since she restored her body's pH balance, she's experienced some amazing results. In the course of a conversation with her, she said (and these are her words), "I can walk again!"** And I said, "What did you say?" She repeated, "I can walk again!" Then she started telling me about how her legs had been so bad before the treatment that she could hardly walk.

That became the headline for my test ad: "I can walk again!" It's designed to be exciting and catch the reader's attention—which you absolutely have to do, because so much of the marketing out there is just plain boring, and people find it easy to ignore. They have to ignore something, after all, since they're being bombarded with so many messages so constantly.

As I pointed out earlier, **bored people don't buy.** Neither do those who missed your message because they weren't paying attention. **The only people who buy are those you've interested and excited.** So it's up to you to find those biggest benefits in whatever you're selling and convey them to the prospect in the most dramatic way. Give them a story as exciting and hopeful as Mary being able to walk again. They're really going to pay attention to that.

Last but not least, I'll say this: **Start paying close attention to your own emotions.** What excites you when you read other people's ads and sales copy? Use those features as a model. **The marketing materials that get you excited can teach you how to transfer that excitement to your own material, if you take the time to really study them.**

CHAPTER FIVE

The value of an employee is determined by 2 things:

1. How much money they <u>directly</u> bring into the company? (In other words, without their <u>direct</u> effort — this money would not have come in.)

2. How difficult will they be to replace?

Nothing else matters.

Know the Value
of a Good Employee

This statement is a bit controversial, I'm afraid. In fact, the only time I've ever had my father-in-law mad at me (that I know of), to the point where he turned about three shades of red, is when I told him what I'm going to tell you now. Now, understand that I've always had a good relationship with my father-in-law. But when I expressed this concept to him one day, he acted like he wanted to come right across the table and hit me as hard as he could. If looks could kill, I would have been in the hospital at least!

So here it is. The value of an employee is determined by two things: 1) how much money they directly bring in to the company, and 2) how difficult they are to replace. Nothing else matters. As repugnant as that might seem to some, this is the harsh reality.

My father-in-law got so angry with me when I said that because he was from the old school, where your value as an employee was determined by how many years you'd been with the company. But I don't believe that at all, and I told him so bluntly. There are people who have been with their companies for 10 and 20 years who aren't really contributing to the company; they're just going through the motions. They're no better now than when they started. I told my father-in-law that those people don't deserve to get paid any more money than they got paid the first year, because they're not contributing at a higher level... and boy, he got pissed at me! All of his life, **he was taught that your value should increase, no matter what, for every year that you stayed with the company. But that's nonsense.** All an employee's value really boils down to is their contribution and how difficult it would be to replace them. If you can get rid of them tomorrow without affecting the company one iota, then how valuable are they, really?

I know that attitude is unpopular. But let me repeat: **if you can get rid of an employee tomorrow, and the business keeps running just as smoothly, how much value really do they have?** Zero! Every employee at a company should be able to make the case that they're making money for the company. In my company, I look for people who can make money that the company would never have made without them.

Case in point: We have a sales department run by a gentleman named Drew Hansen. We call Drew's crew Client Service Representatives, but really what they are is salespeople. Now, being a salesperson kind of has a bad rap, because a few bad apples have helped make the whole batch seem rotten. In a recent sales meeting, I pointed out, "There are a lot of people running around claiming to be marketers because they're ashamed to call themselves salespeople." But look: **salespeople directly earn the company money, so they're valuable.** It's not that those people in the company who directly generate revenue are better than everyone else at a social level; it's just that they're more valuable *to the company*. They're generating revenue the company would not have enjoyed without them.

I know for a fact that Chris Lakey, our marketing director, has generated millions of dollars for our company through the ideas that he's come up with. Without those ideas, the company would never have generated those millions. I know that for a *fact*. So Chris is much more valuable than some rank-and-file employee who comes to work, puts in his time, keeps his head down, and goes home. That's just reality. It's not that Chris is a better person overall than that hypothetical time-server. It's not about moral superiority at all. His great value to M.O.R.E., Inc. emerges from the fact that without him, those millions he brought in would not have existed.

Think about that. Such people are extremely valuable, and they're difficult, if not impossible, to replace. Therefore, those people deserve to make more money than others in the company. Now, this can be a sore subject within any workplace. Everyone wants others to recognize their value and worth. **I've got 26 full-time employees right now, and I value all of them.** They're very, very good people, they're honest, they work hard—and they'd all like to make more money. And yes, the people at the very top of the company do make good money.

But the flat fact of the matter is that no matter how good and honest my employees are, there are some who would be very easy to replace if I had to, in large part because they don't directly generate much (if any) income independently for the company. They're replaceable cogs in the corporate machine. No one wants to feel that way, and they especially don't want to know that that's how they're seen by management; so it becomes a sore subject. If I were a politician, there's no way I'd be writing this down! I know how the discussion affects a lot of people. After all, the only time my father-in-law wanted to throttle me, over the course of my 23 years of marriage, was because of my views on this subject.

Frankly, this subject is difficult to talk about with just about anyone, because most people are employees. Very few are employers. Most people feel like they have value to their company, that they're a valuable part of a team. **It's a big part of who they are. So when you talk about their value as an employee, you strike at the very heart of their ego.**

To be more philosophical, what *is* a job? What is labor? These kinds of questions, I think, are important—especially today, because (at least as I'm writing this), our economy is not doing well. Everybody's talking about jobs, and unemployment is high. A lot of politicians try to fix things by creating job programs, or by otherwise creating incentives for employers to hire more people. **But to do that well, you have to go back to employment at its basic core level: why do jobs exist? If you answer that question, then you find the value of an employee.**

I think that ultimately, the reason a job exists is because a company, person, or individual needs something done. The job doesn't really exist for the benefit of the employee. Leaving all social factors aside, an individual's value as an employee is balanced against what you have to pay them in terms of dollars. If you have to pay them $20 an hour, you need to get at least that much value in return from their services. **Hopefully, they'll bring in (or at least save) much more money than they cost you.** If they don't, you have a decision to make about whether or not you need to replace them... and remember, you run a *business*, not a social support service. **Labor is a cost; and you've got to keep your costs as low as you can. That's part of the whole secret of profitability.**

That means you have to count an employee's cost just like you'd count any other cost in your business, weigh that cost against their performance, and determine whether it's profitable for you to continue to have that person doing the job. **The point of having an employee in the first place is *not* to help someone out; you offer someone a job because you need something done, and you believe they can do it for you.** Now, all that said, I don't think of people as *just* costs. My employees aren't just numbers on a balance sheet to me. But the fact is that some employees deserve to be paid more money, because of what they do and how much money they directly make for the company.

I know this is an unpopular message. I'm glad that my father-in-law didn't do what it looked like he wanted to do to me when we discussed the subject, because I love the man. But he grew up with what I think is an outdated idea. It was valid in the days of the union, but corporate expediency is putting an end to the hold that seniority has on labor markets. Even so, **there are still too many long-term employees who aren't doing anything more today than they were doing 10 years ago**— and as a result, they don't contribute much to the bottom-line profits, and don't deserve to get paid the big bucks just because they've held on.

Your pay should be based on your merits and value to the company. Enough said.

CHAPTER SIX

The right stories will easily warm people up and prepare them for the close.

Choose the Right Stories

You've got to use the right stories in your marketing copy, in order to warm people up and prepare them for the close. So many marketers stumble on this point; they could and should be telling more stories, but they simply don't. **People want to hear stories; they *love* to hear stories.** Consider the story I just told you about my father-in-law; didn't that pique your interest?

People like analogies. They like comparisons. When somebody says, "Hey, I want to tell you a funny story," all of a sudden you perk up a little, don't you? You want to hear about it. The best teachers, preachers, commentators, salesmen, and politicians tell a lot of stories. **And if you pay close attention, you'll see that they try to intertwine their message within the story.** Instead of coming right out and saying, "Here are the five biggest benefits of my product or service," **they might tell a story about how somebody benefited from their product or service...** like the story I'm preparing to tell about my graphic artist, Mary Jones.

I've already mentioned Mary's issue earlier. **The new health product we're selling helps people restore their pH balance and keep it in line.** Thanks to this product, Mary can walk again without pain. It's a before-and-after story, which is ideal for the selling environment: **"Before, I was in terrible pain when I tried to walk. And then I got my pH balance restored, and now all of a sudden I can walk again and I'm feeling so much**

better!" Before-and-after stories work like gangbusters. They sell. They make a difference. **They influence people.**

Look at a good ad for a weight-loss product: you'll see testimonial after testimonial. Why? Because stories sell! **Most of us distrust marketers and salespeople per se, but we'll listen to stories that other people tell us** — especially if they're dramatic stories where somebody experienced a real benefit. Those stories influence us like almost nothing else can.

And really, what we're talking about when discussing marketing is influencing and persuading people. You know that people don't really want to be sold anything; I've discussed that before. People are naturally resistant to hard sells; they're aware that any salesman or marketer they face is just trying to get them to give up their money. Any of us only has so much money to spend — **so the marketplace is a kind of tug-of-war battle. Stories can help you break down the prospect's resistance.** It's an indirect way of selling, because you're hiding your sales message in the story, making your points in a roundabout way and telling people things they want to hear.

And remember: people buy with their emotions, so you have to reach them emotionally; and there's no better way to do it than with a story.

Stories have been used to convey messages throughout history. Jesus used parables and stories, as you can read in the Bible. Stage performers and presenters also tell lots of stories. Chris Lakey was at a concert recently, and the leader of the band was constantly telling stories between songs — where the song came from, what it was about, why he wrote it. That sort of thing can endear you to the person telling the story.

We tell our own stories in our marketing—especially the story of how my wife and I first got started in the business. **In many markets—especially the opportunity market—people want to know who they're dealing with.** Most prospects are in this marketplace because they want to make more money, which usually means they're unhappy with the money they're currently making. **They're struggling, so they can identify with our true story of struggling until we found a moneymaking system that worked.** The story rings true to them; it's their own story. When people hear it from us, they feel like they have a relationship with us. **They understand where we came from, because that's where *they* come from.** And they feel that if Eileen and I can do it, then they can do it!

If you're selling a weight loss product and you say, "Here's my story about my struggle with weight… and then I found this natural product, and within 30 days I lost this much weight and gained more energy," that appeals to others who are trying to lose weight. **They can identify with the story; it warms them up, helping you build a bond at an emotional level.** It's hard to quantify exactly how this works, but it really does happen.

And so, whether you're selling from a platform, over the telephone, in a newspaper ad, or by mail, you need to use stories to convey your message and illustrate your points. **You'll find the sales coming easier as your relationships with your customers improve, ultimately becoming more profitable.** That's your goal, after all: to develop a long-lasting relationship

that you can both profit from.

People prefer to do business with folks they share some common ground with. That's why the Eileen and T.J. Rohleder story has generated millions of dollars for us... though to be honest, we've told it so often that I'm sick of it! I still tell it, but not like I used to; and I really should be telling it more often, because people like to hear it. It's just that I'm thinking, *My God, am I going to be 60 years old and still telling that story about what happened when I was 28 and my wife was 30*? And in any case, I don't necessarily like talking about myself as much as some people think I do.

But I can't escape or ignore the fact that stories bond people. Eileen and I have a very dramatic story that resonates with the stories of so many other people in the opportunity market. We used to send away for all those moneymaking plans and programs. We were dead broke constantly. Our friends and family all laughed at us and told us we were crazy. Some of them begged us to stop sending for all the get-rich-quick plans and programs. **They called us "fools," and we took a lot of abuse from people** like one friend who basically told me, "Look, T.J., you can still come over to my house if you want. But if you ever try to sell me another moneymaking opportunity, our friendship is dissolved. That's it."

Of course, we had the last laugh. **We refused to give up; we kept believing in ourselves, and we found a few good people who helped us, like Russ von Hoelscher, and we went on to make millions of dollars in no time flat.** That's our whole story—the 60-second version. Even at that length, it's an effective before-and-after story: here's the way our life was before, here's what happened, and here's our life today.

A lot of movies are plotted exactly that way. One of my staff, Jeremy Webster, is a movie critic; he writes all kinds of articles on the subject. He tells me that films almost all start with a "before" situation—here's the way things are right now. Then something dramatic happens, and here's what happens afterwards. As he points out, most movies begin placidly; then something goes catastrophically wrong, and everybody spends the rest of the movie trying to adapt to it. That's the basis of a good story. **You have to give your main characters a conflict that challenges them in a significant way.** The real story comes from showing how they respond to the conflict—and there's always a nemesis of some sort, even if it's just the conflict itself.

Well, in marketing you need to share the same nemesis with your prospects to be effective. As they say, "the enemy of my enemy is my friend." Instant friendship! **The collective nemesis in our story, at least in part, is the group of opportunity publishers and marketers who ripped us off for years.** They lied to us, they cheated us, they misled us, they sold us a bunch of crap—**and then, when we needed support and guidance, they were nowhere to be found.** They were using fake addresses and phony names. They weren't even real people, just quasi-criminal fly-by-nighters. We tell that story because, again, it's a frustration we share with the millions of people in the opportunity market.

Because people want to do business with people who are just like them, now that we're entering into the health market I've changed my story. **Now I tell people in my sales literature**

about how I spend hundreds of dollars a month on dietary supplements. I'm not telling them I'm a millionaire; I'm just trying to reach them on our common ground. I'm saying, "Look, I love taking all these supplements. **I wanted to get my supplements for free every month, and I was thinking maybe you felt the same way."** I want to present them with something we share. Again, as a marketer, **you have to look for commonalities like that to warm people up for the close.**

Now, the close is just what you do at the end of the sales pitch to finally get paid. It's the time of decision-making, when you're asking the prospect to give you the money in exchange for what you're offering. In order for that to happen, certain things have to occur first. Stories lay the groundwork for the close by soothing suspicions. Remember, most people come into a negotiation untrusting, and unwilling to spend money. **They become open and receptive only after you've done the right things, after you've built those bonds with them.**

Let's take a quick look at our new Yoli opportunity as an example. The five people who founded this company wanted to get into the nutritional drink market because it's so popular. Plenty of MLM companies have already generated bazillions of dollars with liquid nutrition, so the Yoli group needed something to help make them distinctive in the eyes of the public. Therefore, they tell their story like this: When they decided to build their own company, they went to one of the biggest liquid nutrition products manufacturers in the entire world, and took a tour of their factory. This place was state-of-the-art, and cost hundreds of millions of dollars to set up. As they were taking the tour, they came across this huge machine that took up an entire room.

They asked the tour guide, "What is that huge machine?" And she said, "That's our pasteurizer. The liquid has to go through a pasteurization process before we bottle it." **By the way, every liquid drink sold has to undergo pasteurization, which involves heating and processing the liquid to eliminate bacteria and other toxic growths.** Well, they understood about pasteurization, so they asked her, "Isn't some of the nutrition lost through the heating process? And she admitted that it was; in fact, she said, "A lot of the nutritional elements are just cooked right out."

The Yoli investors immediately decided they couldn't go with a process that robbed their drink of its nutritional value. Instead, they put their heads together and came up with a process that retains that nutrition. **Yoli takes the form of a granulated freeze-dried powder that you mix on the spot before you drink it, so you get all the nutritional aspects of the drink, just as they intended.** None of it's lost in a pasteurization process.

Now, I'll admit that I don't tell that story as well as Robbie Fender, the CEO of the company that produces Yoli. When he presents it, the story really has legs; it gets to you emotionally. **You immediately see Yoli's competitive advantage over all those pasteurized liquid nutrition products out there.** If you care about your health, that story can make money for them.

Storytelling is quite simply one of the easiest ways to get your message across, and at the same time endear yourself to your marketplace. You know, when you're having a beer with a buddy or drinking tea with a friend, you always tell stories. In business, it should be no different. **Storytelling is**

a part of life, and it's a part of business. The more you can use stories, the more likely you are to build the bond that helps make a sale. Usually, people don't do business with people they don't know, though there are exceptions — you go to McDonald's you pick up a burger whether you know the person at the counter or not, for example. **But in general, business is based on relationships. If you can build a relationship with your prospect, you build a bridge to the sale. Period.** So use stories to help you: not just the first time you do business with someone, but all the other times as well. Continuously use stories to help convey your messages.

I want to wrap this up with the tale of a simple story that literally made a billion dollars for the advertiser. It was just a two-page Direct Mail letter for *The Wall Street Journal,* which they used as a control letter to sell subscriptions for two decades. No matter how many letters they tested it against, it always made more money. No other copywriter could beat it.

That two-page letter told a very simple story: Two guys who went to the same college go to their class reunion 25 years later. They both had the same Grade Point Average, and they're both the same age; but one of these guys is a CEO of a large company. He's super-successful and rich; he's really done something with his life. He's got the nice houses and cars and vacations, and a bank account full of money. The other guy's a mid-level manager living in a not-so-nice neighborhood, and barely has enough money to send his kids to good colleges. He's always suffered financially.

And then they point out that **the only real difference**

between these two gentlemen is that the more successful one subscribes to the *Wall Street Journal,* while the other does not. The subscriber was kept informed of all the latest and greatest technological breakthroughs, not to mention the best ways to handle his money and get ahead, and so he was always on the cutting edge. As a result, he was far and away the more successful of these two otherwise identical men. Now, which of the two do *you* want to be? **You want to be the guy who went to the top, of course!** So, by God, all you have to do is subscribe to *Wall Street Journal* and BOOM, there it is right there! Now *you* can be the guy who has a few million dollars in his bank account, who never has to worry about money again, who lives in the lap of luxury.

If you think about it, it's kind of a dumb story. And yet, that letter ultimately generated a billion dollars worth of sales for the *Wall Street Journal.* They kept trying to beat it with other controls, too; that's part of what you do to make money in Direct Mail. **No matter how good your piece is, you always want to see if you can make it better.** For two decades, they hired the best copywriters in the world to try to beat it, and no one could. That story resonated with business people. They loved it, and they bought the *Journal* because they wanted to be the guy with everything.

Stories work. They reach people emotionally, and make sales where sales wouldn't happen otherwise. **So look for those dramatic stories, and tell them in the best way you can.** If you do it right, you can be just like that successful guy in the *Wall Street Journal* story—you can have it all!

CHAPTER SEVEN

❧❦❧

"You must enter the conversation that's already in their mind."

— *Robert Collier*

Enter the Conversation Already in Their Mind

This is based on a quote from Robert Collier, one of the greatest marketers who ever lived. The full quote goes like this: **"You must enter the conversation that's already in their mind."** That seems simple enough, right? And yet, so many marketers and salespeople just miss the boat on this one.

Empathy is crucial from a marketing perspective — empathy being, of course, a deep understanding of how your prospects are thinking and feeling. You have to know them intimately, to the point that you instinctively know what their unconscious buying decisions will be. In other words, you not only know why they're buying the kinds of products and services you sell, but you also know what to say to them that lets them know that you understand their hopes and dreams, and that you can identify with the pains and frustrations they're going through. **Furthermore, knowing their biggest objections to your products — their sticking points, as it were — is vital.**

A deep comprehension of the marketplace will win you sales. And getting there is a learning process; like anything else, the longer you're in the market, and the more you think things through, the better you're going to get at understanding what makes your prospects and customers tick. **Nothing is more powerful than getting inside people's heads and hearts and really understanding them.**

Just thinking things through takes a lot of time on your part. **That's one of the reasons why we strongly suggest that you choose a marketplace you already have an intimate understanding of**—a marketplace that you yourself have bought from or do buy from, representing a hobby that interests you a great deal, or a line of products and services that excites you greatly, so that you'll naturally develop a keener awareness of yourself—which will translate to a better awareness of your marketplace. **This deep understanding allows you to enter the conversations in your customer's mind, since you know exactly where they're coming from.**

Like most of our Ways, this one sounds like common sense—and yet marketers continue to make the same few mistakes here. **Many don't answer objections at all;** they just assume that the customer is going to believe whatever they say. **They do nothing to alleviate the fears and concerns of their prospects, and have never really taken the time to understand what their customers want more than anything else.** They tend to assume that just because they're excited about a certain product or service, the customers are going to feel the same way. That does help, and sometimes they get lucky; but the people who make the most money consistently are the ones who do just what this quote suggests. They enter the conversation already underway in the prospect's mind.

Remember, it's all about *them*. What are their biggest concerns? What do they care about the most? What are they thinking about the most? What do they want more than anything else in the world? What's different about the people in your market? What are they searching for that no one else is giving them? What can you *give* them that nobody else is giving them? How can you learn how to think more like they do? How can you connect with them in the most powerful way?

One of the ways we've been able to connect effectively to the people in our marketplace, thereby entering the conversations in their minds and thoroughly relating to them, is by telling our rags-to-riches story. I don't tell that story enough these days. In fact, recently, one of our seminar clients wondered why I *wasn't* telling our story. He sat there all day long; and then, as Chris and I were closing out the seminar, the subject came up... and I just had to say, "Oh my goodness, I'm so sick of that story. I just can't stand it anymore!" But the thing is, the prospects and customers like to hear it. **They have a deep need to be understood; they desperately want to connect with other people whom they feel understand them.**

That's why we tell our story about the years when we were broke and frustrated and confused, and how we came out of that by persevering, ignoring our critics, and getting capable, competent, honest help. **We became millionaires within a few short years, and now we've dedicated our lives to helping other people who are just like we used to be. That's why we tell it, and that's why it works.** Now, that's a very plain, brief version of our story; but when I tell it in a more dramatic way, going into detail about each of those things that I just outlined so quickly, the story is magic. It has literally made us millions of dollars. It's built relationships and connected us with thousands of people, because it does exactly what Robert Collier teaches us in his quote.

When Collier says, "Enter the conversation that's in their

mind," he's talking about making deep connections with people, to the point that they really do feel that you know them— because you're speaking their language. Essentially, our story is so powerful because it's a before-and-after story; that factor is central to every good story, not just in marketing but in the rest of life as well. **Here's where we were *before*, and here are all the problems associated with that situation; then something happens, and that serves as a bridge to the *after* situation.** Everybody wants to be in the *after* part of the story. When we tell our story, we reveal to our prospects the fact that we've gone through and overcome the same problems they're going through. So they really identify with us; we're in their heads and hearts now. We're connecting with them. **We *are* them! We tell that story because it's also their story, and when we tell it, we enter the conversation already going on in their heads.**

So do all you can to build empathy and thus to build your relationship with your prospects, to let them know that you're a real person like they are—and then do all you can to answer all their fears and objections.

Too many sales letters and promotions ignore that last suggestion. They don't bother to address the skepticism and the doubts that people have. And believe me, people have a lot of doubts! It's a rare individual who just buys anything without reservations. **You have to understand and accept that most people don't believe a single word you're saying.** Now, that statement isn't meant be negative; but it's indicative of reality. **If you start with that as your basic premise, you'll be ahead of the pack.** Realize and accept that the average consumer's mind is filled with all kinds of doubts and fears and disbeliefs. **Your** goal is to do everything possible to counter them — to convince the prospect that everything you're saying is the truth, the whole truth, and nothing but. You have to mean it, too, and you need to have all kinds of protections in place so that if the things that they're worried about do occur, they'll still end up winners. **You want them to perceive that all the chips are stacked on their side of the table, not yours.**

Therefore, part of entering the conversation in the prospect's mind is realizing, at an instinctual level, that they're inherently skeptical — and that they've got every reason to be. **Since they're already skeptical, you might as well just nail it right away.** In our sales literature, we're very upfront about that. We tell people flat out, "Look, don't take our word for it. We don't expect you to believe what we're saying." And then we actually praise people for being skeptical. **Don't run from it or hide from it.** We say, "If you're not skeptical in this day and age, you're going to get lied to, you're going to be cheated, you're going to be ripped off — you're going to be abused by people intent on taking advantage of you." They already know that, and we don't pretend otherwise.

Then we try to create offers where they come out smelling like a rose in the end; they'll still winners, even in a worst-case scenario. Consider our recent year-end push for 2011. We offered to give our prospects two Amazon Kindle book readers. These are phenomenal devices! As I write this, they're still new, they're still exciting, and they offer all kinds of benefits our prospects crave.

Our offer was simple. Knowing that our prospects were filled with fears, doubts, concerns, disbelief, and skepticism — as all prospects for anything are these days—**the offer was that if they would sign up immediately for this special position we were making available to them, they could keep the Kindles no matter what.** They even had a month or so to decide whether they were in or out... and if they decided that they were out, then we would not only give them every penny back, but we would let them keep the Kindles.

So we weren't running from their skepticism. We knew that they were skeptical, as all modern consumers are. We knew that they had their doubts. We knew that they were being pitched to by our competitors, too; and, in fact, we also told them that, right up front. We said, "We're more than happy to give this to you, because we know you're looking at all kinds of other opportunities—and we just want you to consider ours. We want to make sure this is better than no-risk." No-risk is where they just get their money back, you see. **This was better than no-risk, because it gave them their money back,** *plus* **let them keep two great free gifts that we knew they'd like.**

We knew what to do here because we had entered the collective conversation already occurring in their minds, rather than running or hiding from it.

Now, you have to realize that this mental conversation does change from time to time. It evolves, occasionally taking on a different tone or direction according to mood, situation, or the season in an individual's life. But whatever the case may be at a particular moment, that inner conversation trumps almost all other activity and thought, and it drives them through whatever they're experiencing. Let's say they're out of a job, struggling financially—unsure of where the next rent or mortgage payment

90

is coming from, much less how they'll deal with the loss of their health insurance. These financial concerns consume them, and are very top-of-mind.

Or suppose they're focused on buying their next car. In this case, the inner conversion is usually dominated by the question, "Where am I going to find the best deal?" In this example, the inner conversation is market-based as well as situation-based. If someone's actively in the market for something, that's the primary conversation going on in their head. **As marketers, we have to enter that conversation as smoothly and effectively as we can, and take advantage of the fact that the individual is already focused on something important to them.** Then we can position ourselves to serve them best.

It's easy to see the "inner conversation" concept in action in a busy family situation. Chris Lakey, my Marketing Director and sidekick, has six kids at home, ranging in age from 4½ to almost 15. There are lots of internal conversations happening in all these age groups—and there's plenty of external talking going on, too. Internal or external, those conversations represent what's primary in the kids' minds at any particular moment. All Chris' kids have things that are important to them, varying from kid to kid. His oldest daughter is a freshman in high school, so her conversations are about school. She's concerned about grades, she worries about her interaction with teachers, and she thinks about all the activities going on at school and church. All those things are important to her.

Chris also has a 13-year-old son, and his conversations are similar, but different. He's interested in drums and he likes sports, especially soccer—he'll talk about soccer all day long if you let him. But he has school issues as well. And then Chris's 10-year-old daughter has *her* concerns that dominate her thoughts... and the list goes on, all the way down to his four year old, whose concerns are unique and all over the place.

All of them have conversations underway in their minds. **Like all of us, they're fixated on the things that are important to them, and they try to express those things constantly in verbal conversations with their parents and others.** If you've ever had a child, then you know very well that this is true. It doesn't matter what the subject matter is, whatever's in their head at that moment is the most important thing on the planet, and it has to be said. Needless to say, that tendency dampens somewhat as they grow a little older.

The point is, to really get through to someone, you have to tap into whatever is of utmost importance to that person. To do so, you have to know them so well that you can easily get on their radar and get noticed. **Hit them when the conversation you're interested in is *the* most important thing in their life at that moment; and like I said, it does change from time to time.** If someone loses a job, all of a sudden employment is going to be top- of-mind to them. If they're trying to lose a hundred pounds because their doctor said they'd die if they didn't, weight loss is at the top of their mind. That drives them to a specific marketplace; so if someone is shopping in your marketplace, you know that they're interested in doing business with you. You know the conversation they're having in their mind, so you have to address that, and everything associated with it, head-on.

That's why we immediately address the skepticism that

people in our marketplace inevitably feel. **We'd be pretty foolish to do otherwise—because if we don't at least mention it, it's not going to disappear.** It'll just get worse because we've refused to address it. Ultimately, we produce a much better result in the end by just bringing it up and talking about it.

Another thing to remember about the conversations going on in the minds of your prospects is that those conversations are usually desire-driven or action-driven. The prospects are searching for a result, trying to address a desire for a certain outcome. If someone has a sincere desire to lose weight, that desire drives the conversation in their mind. If someone sincerely wants to make money, moneymaking success drives the conversation in their mind. So beyond basics like socks and groceries (and you have some leeway even there), the conversation going on in the mind of an average consumer is usually based on desire—even if it's as simple as the desire to be free of annoyance.

Now, Robert Collier also had something very interesting to say about desire: "Plant the seed of desire in your mind, and it forms a nucleus with power to attract to itself everything needed for its fulfillment. **The first principle of success is desire— knowing what you want.** Desire is the planting of your seed. **Very few persons know how to desire with efficient intensity.** They do not know what it is to feel and manifest that intense, eager longing, craving, insistent, demanding, ravenous desire, which is akin to the persistent, insistent, ardent, overwhelming desire of the drowning man for a breath of air, of the shipwrecked or desert-lost man for a drink of water, or of the famished man for bread and meat."

Consider this from your own personal experience. **If you keenly desire success, the intensity of that desire is what drives you to make money and do well in business.** So you could look at it that way; consider how the conversation in your own head is going. **Then shift to your prospect's perspective.** The conversation going on in their mind is probably very intense: it's very eager, very longing, craving, insistent, demanding—it's ravenous. Think about the prospect you're trying to reach with your advertising. Think about the things they want, the things that are most important to them. Earlier, I used the example of Chris Lakey's kids. Well, when they're ardent and insistent, when the conversations in their heads are driving them unceasingly, they won't give up until Chris stops and pays attention to them. They just want the conversation. They want to tell Chris something that's of utmost importance to them.

It's the same way with your prospects, and the conversations they're having in *their* minds. **Those conversations are of utmost importance to them; and if you don't address those conversations, you'll miss out on the opportunity to connect with them at the level needed to sell to them.**

Remember this the next time you're crafting an offer, writing a sales letter, producing an audio program, selling from a platform on stage, or whatever you're doing to reach your marketplace. **Think about the things that are most important to your prospects—the conversations going on in their heads—and you'll be much more likely to make a connection with them.** The right connection is crucial to binding those people to you and making the sale.

CHAPTER EIGHT

Every great story has two essential elements: TENSION & DISCOVERY.

It's all about pressure and release! Build the pressure, create the tension, make it real, and <u>then introduce the discovery</u>! *Now you can sell them!*

Apply Tension and Discovery to Your Stories

Every great story has two essential elements: tension and discovery. It's all about pressure and release. **You build the pressure, you create the tension, you make it real, and then you introduce the discovery so you can sell it to the listeners.**

As I've outlined in previously, the very best salespeople and marketers know how to tell great stories that help illustrate the points they're trying to make, and help answer all the prospect's objections—passing underneath their radar in the process. **These marketers tell a lot of stories, because doing so reaches people emotionally, assuming they can do it correctly.** That's why a good storyteller makes an extra effort to get the point across in ways people are more apt to listen to. People simply love to hear a good story, and so they love good storytellers.

Some people are better at storytelling than others, **but it's a learnable ability.** We can all get better at it, if we just practice and become more consciously aware of what we have to do to transfer our own emotions to the audience.

One of our good friends, Russ von Hoelscher, is an amazing storyteller. He fills his stories with so much detail and he tells them in such a great way that you can see that he really enjoys laying the whole story out, building it up, and then delivering the punchline at the end. I've known Russ now for over 20 years, so I've heard some of his best stories dozens of times; but that doesn't make them any less interesting to listen to. In fact, we'll get together and, because everybody loves hearing his stories, I'll say, "Hey Russ, tell the story about this... " He then launches into the tale, sometimes adding more details this time than last, but managing to make that story so enjoyable that he just rivets my attention... even though I've heard the story many times.

This ability to command attention and transfer emotion with your stories is crucial in a selling environment, because prospects put up all kinds of sales resistance. **They don't want to be sold anything.** They know you're trying to get them to give up their hard-earned money. They also know that they only have so much money to spend, so in their minds, they're worried about making the wrong decision and going broke if they do. **And still, they'll hear you out if you can catch their attention, because they're still looking for the kinds of benefits that your products and services provide.**

This is especially true if they're on your mailing/customer list because you've pre-qualified them. If they've bought items similar to yours in the past, or if they've responded to one of your two-step lead generation ads, you can assume that they *are* qualified prospects—that they're really looking for whatever it is you sell. **And yet at the same time, they're human. They're harboring doubts, skepticism, fears, and objections, and all the other ingredients that come together to form that shield of sales resistance.** And so at some level, they're not really listening to your sales pitch; they know you want them to give up some of their money, and they don't want to. The only way you can actually get them to give up their money is to make then open and receptive to your offer. **You've got to get them to the point where they're really interested in hearing you.**

So you tell stories that illustrate certain points that are important to your overall message of the benefits you're providing—the things that make your company different from all the others. **The best stories to tell are your personal stories.** Sometimes you've got to add a little drama to make the stories more compelling—apply a little "artistic license," so to speak. Now, you don't want to lie to people; it's not about scamming your prospects. But it *is* about trying to make the story interesting, which sometimes doesn't happen easily in real life. While everybody loves stories, nobody loves a *boring* story. **People like a story that offers not just some enthusiasm, but some excitement as well.** So ratchet up the tension to your stories.

That tension can stem from some problem that frustrated you, or a problem that has frustrated a typical buyer. The latter is especially useful, since your prospects can identify with other prospects, people who have had the same exact concerns that your current prospects have. So don't hesitate to bring up those kinds of stories, because they divert skepticism.

Here's a brief excpt from a great story: our own M.O.R.E., Inc. story, the multimillion-dollar rags-to-riches tale of how my wife, Eileen, and I spent so many years searching for the perfect way to get rich. We were on all these different mailing lists, so I'd come home from work every day—from a job I hated!—and my mailbox would be jam-packed with sales letters from people who promised that they could sell me a moneymaking plan that would end all my problems forever. Well, most of these moneymaking programs were pure garbage—not even worth the paper they were printed on. Somebody came up with an idea, and quickly wrote up a plan. **They'd never tested it and had never made any money with it; they were only making money by selling the plan to others.** Well, I didn't know that at the time... and so I spent all my money on moneymaking plans that were essentially worthless. And I was very, very broke.

My friends and family kept telling me that I was crazy, that these opportunity marketers were just ripping me off by making promise after promise and then not fulfilling on any of them. Some of my family members begged me to stop. And yet, we persevered; we continued to believe in our big dreams, which told us it *was* possible to get rich, no matter our circumstances. **We learned a lot along the way, and we refused to give up.** Ultimately, because we didn't quit, and because we found a few people in the marketplace who were honest and sincere and who made their money by helping us make *our* money, we finally got involved in the right opportunities.

Lo and behold, within just a few short years we were millionaires. **Within five, we had brought in a grand total of over ten million dollars. We've never looked back.** Now we've had the last laugh over all of our friends and family, and since that time we've been dedicated to helping other people who are *exactly* like we were for so many years.

That's a slightly longer version of our story than I

sometimes tell, but I hope you can see that there was some tension built up there. It could be played upon more, and I've done so in the past, on occasions when I went into more detail about getting ripped off and lied to and cheated by all the opportunity promoters who were selling us nothing but worthless garbage and empty dreams… **people who wouldn't even give us a refund if we were unhappy with their programs. And then there's the tension from all the family and friends who were laughing at us behind our backs**—and sometimes even laughing right to our faces and telling us that we were crazy, that we were foolish, that we were idiots!

And then there's the tension due to the fact that as we were dealing with all this stuff, we continued to persevere. And then there's discovery at the end—where we found this group of honest people to help us… which really did happen, by the way. None of this is made up. Sometimes we do add a little drama to it, but you can see that it's all about the tension and the discovery. **And in the end, the discovery is what all the prospects want. They're looking for solutions! That's what stories illustrate more than anything else.**

And that's what people buy: results. They have to believe that your product, service, or opportunity fixes their problems; and in order to demonstrate that it does, you have to take them through all those problems first. The story I just told about our company's history resonates with millions of people, because they see their own struggles, their problems, in ours. They're sending away for all the different programs, they're trying all the things that aren't working, they're frustrated, their families and friends are telling them they're crazy. When we tell our story right, they identify strongly with us. **This fact breaks the ice and makes them receptive to our sales message. Now they're ready to be sold.** This helps us build bonds and long-term relationships with them. This has been a really, really good story for us. It's made us millions of dollars.

Other good stories have done the same for us. **For example, we were one of the very first companies to sell Internet products and services.** The benefit of the Internet— the result that people are looking for more than any other—is that it provides low-cost and no-cost marketing. **That offers the ability to get your marketing message out there for little or no money.** So, in order to sell these services, we first told our prospects long stories, examples of all of the things they would normally have to do to get their marketing message delivered. **We'd discuss the high cost and go into all the other details, really building it up until people could identify with how terrible the process was going to be. And then we presented our solution.** When you can do that effectively, suddenly all that tension disappears—which does a good job of building the case, and making people see what we need them to see before they're ready to buy what we want to sell them.

We now offer advertising and management services. As part of our promotional materials, more and more often we're illustrating all the different services that we actually provide under one roof by talking a little about all the trouble you'd have to go through to handle all these things yourself. Yes, you can hire individuals to provide each service for you. You can go out and find a company to write your ads for you, or your sales letters, brochures, and other marketing materials. You can pay a graphic artist to design it all for you. You can get a website developer to build a site for you, and copywriters to write the words on those websites that make your products sell, sell, sell. You can find people who will develop all your products for you. You can find people to run your ads, to answer your phone calls, to ship your products, to do your customer service work, to answer your customers' biggest objections and help make the sales. **Or, you can just hire us, and we'll do it *all* for you under one roof, from lead generation to customer service, A to Z!**

That's hugely convenient. In telling the story, by using those examples and building the tension up, we get people to think, "Oh my God, I'd have to pay different people to do all that... Or, I can just sign up with one of these services and presto, they'll do it all for me!" **The lead-in does build the tension, agitating their worries before offering that discovery, which is a big relief. They just give us their money and let us take care of it all under one roof.** The story helps establish the value, it helps people see everything that they're getting for their money, and it helps make the price we're charging pale by comparison to what they might otherwise pay.

There's nothing that can clinch a sale like a story, especially when combined with the use of specific examples. It's all very, very emotional. And if you do it right, most prospects won't even see that you're doing it. Call that manipulative if you like; I just call it selling. If you really have something that delivers on your promises, something that will benefit others and give them what they want, then you're not lying to anybody. **So any sales method is legitimate, as long as it's legal and doesn't involve physical coercion.**

Now, some sellers *do* use subtle physical coercion, which is despicable. They put prospects in seminar rooms, for example, and then refuse to let them have bio-breaks or meal breaks, and keep them up till three in the morning, and then try to sell to them. That's pushing it a little too far. But again, just about everything else is perfectly acceptable, as long as you really do have something that can benefit your prospects.

But getting back to storytelling: **one reason this tactic works so well is that telling stories is an integral part of life, really.** We tell stories all the time when we're not selling. Maybe you just got back from a great fishing trip, and the first thing you want to do is tell everybody about all the fish you caught and how you got the sunburn that's visible on your face and your arms. People want to know what's going on, and you tell them a story in full detail. That story is part of who you are at that point.

Business is a lot like life. You're busily building relationships with people either way, and the relationships provide value to each party. Of course, in the business relationship you're exchanging money for benefits, while in a personal relationship you're exchanging other things in mutually beneficial terms. The point is, **a lot of the things that are important to you in life are also important to you in business, given that you have to build, cultivate, and maintain relationships with customers in order to provide ongoing profit opportunities.**

The big difference between story telling in your personal and business lives lies in the results you expect. In your personal sphere, you might tell a story about anything and everything:

sports, recreation, hobbies, your kids, whatever. There doesn't necessarily have to be a point. **But in business, you really need to stick to stories that convey your message and move your prospect closer to a sale.** Your stories need to stay focused on the mission—and that's where this strategy of tension and discovery comes into play. Most likely, you're going to be solving some problem that people have with the products and services that you sell.

If you sell a moneymaking opportunity, for example, the problem that people want solved is how they can make more money. At a minimum, they're looking for a nice part-time business that provides extra income. If you're in the health industry, the problem is physical; maybe they have an issue with their weight, or their knees don't work so well anymore. **They've got some condition they need fixed, and they're looking for someone to help them fix it.** That's the problem your story needs to address. If the problem is that the prospect wants to be a better guitar player, for example, then you'd better address that problem in your story.

The problem doesn't have to be large or complex; it could be as simple as needing nails or new underwear (and there are some places where you can buy both). That's what business life is all about. **Businesses provide solutions to problems suffered in a particular marketplace, solutions that prospects are willing to trade their money for.**

Again, your first step with the elements of tension and discovery in business-related storytelling is to first make people aware of a real problem they're experiencing, the pain they're in, the challenge they're facing—and then, ultimately, to make them aware of your solution, which until then they might not have realized actually existed. **You're standing there holding up a sign, pointing the way.**

Now, consider again the importance of entering that conversation that's going on in the prospect's head. They need a solution for their primary problem, and their thoughts are bent on finding that solution. **Sometimes your solution is to ratchet up the tension part of this equation by reminding them of the condition they're in.** Let's say they need money, so at some level they're looking for a moneymaking solution. Maybe their pain stems from the very real possibility that their house is about to be foreclosed on; or maybe they can't make their car payment and it's about to be repossessed, or, even more pressing, their kids are hungry. They have a major problem on their hands!

Is it mean and manipulative to remind them of that problem—to agitate it and make it hurt? Some might say so, but you didn't create their condition; you're just pointing it out to them, reminding them of the pain they're in before you offer the solution. **Pointing out the problem is part of the tension phase of this tactic; the discovery is revealing the solution you have for them.** You illustrate both those points through storytelling. And remember, your stories need to be focused on your mission. That's why you need to bring up the existing problem and agitate it.

There's a formula called "Problem, Agitate, Solution," or PAS, that plays directly into this tactic, and it's easy to adapt when telling your stories. **The first thing is to identify the**

problem, and then you agitate it a little—make it real, make it painful. If they're not in pain, they've got less desire for your solution. And then offer them the third element of the formula, which is the solution to the problem.

You might wonder: what's the point of rubbing salt in someone's wound? Well, let me offer a little example. Let's say I'm doing some work around the house, and I get a little splinter in my finger. The splinter isn't that big a deal to me. It agitated my skin just a little, but it's not enough to stop me from working. I'm aware of it, it's there, it bothers me, but I know it will probably work itself out. In fact, the next time I wash my hands, the action of rubbing my hands under the water with some soap is probably going to agitate that splinter enough that it will pop out. I really don't even have to think much about it, so I really have no need to seek out any solution, other than what's going to happen naturally over time. But if I chop my finger off, I'm in a worse predicament. I need immediate attention to save my finger.

In a sense, you're pointing out to people that they've chopped their fingers off. If I were to injure myself severely, I would hope that someone else would tell me about it and offer a solution to help. **With your marketing, then, all you're doing is pointing out the obvious—reminding them of the condition they're in, and then offering them the solution you have.** If you really do have a solution, then you're doing them a disservice if you don't tell them about their problem and offer your solution. In some cultures, it's actually a crime to sit on the sidelines and allow someone to needlessly suffer when you could have helped.

I'm actually going to use that point in some copy I'm writing. And then I'm going to tell people how they may suffer if they don't get involved in our opportunity, in order to illustrate one of our customers' biggest fears: losing out on something that could have made them a lot of money. That may be stretching the point a bit, but here's the thing: **if you have a solution to someone's problem, then it's valuable to offer that solution to them.** If it just so happens that you make the offer in the confines of a business deal and make a profit from the solution, so what? You shouldn't feel any shame for that.

When you do make that offer, use stories to illustrate that need by winding up the tension before offering the solution. **And the key thing to remember here is that your stories have to be relevant to the selling point.** Otherwise they might get people off track; they might make them focus on the wrong things, and for whatever reason make them decide to seek solutions elsewhere. So you want to be focused, and you want to use your stories to move people along the path of discovery toward your solution. If you use stories in that manner, you'll find them very effective. **Every great story moves you towards sales.**

Look for stories constantly. Study how other people are using them in their marketing. Start looking at this topic more objectively—and get on the other side of the cash register. Even when you have a friend tell a good story, go back and think about what they were doing—how they set everything up, and how they delivered it. To a large degree, it's all about entertaining people. **People want to be entertained; they *need* to be entertained, and they'll reward you if you do it correctly.**

One of my favorite movies is Steve Martin's *Leap of Faith*, which is worth watching and re-watching because it teaches this method so well. People want to be entertained. Now, they don't want to be sold anything; they love stories, but they hate sales pitches. **And yet if they're good, qualified prospects, you know they're looking for whatever it is that you're offering.** So start paying attention to how other people are using this method in their marketing!

I read a lot of books, especially biographies. One of the reasons I love biographies, and read them again and again, is because of the stories they offer. The best biographies bring out the subject's whole story, so you can see everything in your head—like a movie in your mind. It's captivating.

That's what great stories are; fun and entertaining. Learn how to tell them well, add in tension and discovery, and tell more of them. **Learn how to tell stories that sell!**

CHAPTER NINE

An entrepreneurial rule for choosing new ventures:

In any new business venture — if it's not a stretch — don't do it! It must scare you and induce some risk. <u>If not, don't do it</u>.

If It's Not a Stretch,
Then Don't Do It

Here's an entrepreneurial rule of thumb for choosing new business ventures: if the venture isn't a stretch, then don't get involved in it. **It must scare you a little, and induce some risk; otherwise, what's the point?**

I've learned that fear is an interesting thing. I've dealt with an abnormal number of fears, insecurities, and doubts all my life… I've been loaded with them! It's terrible; these are things I've had to struggle with constantly. But I also can tell you that I *have* struggled with them. I've tried to rise above them and I really believe that, for the most part, **you have to make friends with your fear. It has to be a constant traveling companion.** You're never going to get rid of it. When you do start getting rid of it, you've got to take on more risk. **You *have* to have the fear! It's good for you. It's energy. Fear = energy.** And the more something scares you, the more energy you have available.

When you consistently look for ventures that do scare you, that means you're stretching yourself. You're not just doing the same things over and over again. **You're always trying to push for more—always trying to increase your skills and abilities.** You're trying to take your companies in new directions, which is absolutely necessary, because the marketplace is always moving. **The businesspeople who suffer the most are those who continue to do the same things year in and year out.** There's never anything new, never anything exciting, never anything to stimulate the imagination of the marketplace and to stimulate *them*. Then they wonder why their sales and profits are flat. Well, it's because there's not enough innovation in their businesses. They're not reaching, they're not growing, they're not stretching themselves, and they're not doing the kinds of risk-taking things that require a little bit of fear.

You've heard the quote that goes, "No risk, no reward." Or the flipside of that, **"The greater the risk, the greater the reward." The biggest and boldest ideas are the ones that can produce the biggest profits for you.** For example, we have something very bold that we're currently developing. It's called "The Health Resource Portal," and it's going to contain many, many different things. You may have heard of WebMD; well, we're mirroring WebMD for alternative medicine and alternative health. **Our portal will offer a wide variety of resources for people who are serious about their health and are looking for ways to live longer, feel better, have more energy and more vitality, and not suffer from all the deadly diseases that kill so many other people before their time.** That's the kind of people our web portal will attract.

When our clients purchase this web portal from us, among other things they get over 2,400 unique websites as part of the package. Each of those websites sells a health-related product or service in 145 different countries—with no currency exchange problems, no MasterCard or Visa merchant accounts or setup fees, no headaches, no hassles. We're doing it all for them. So this is a huge idea, something that really captivates the imaginations of our prospects. It gets them excited!

Imagine the chance to have 2,400 websites that sell 2,400 different products that are all related to helping people live longer and feel better. **Each one of these products can make them automatic money, and it's all hands-free income for them.** They don't have to do anything! We can do all the marketing, run the marketing systems—and the products are sold for them automatically. **They just sit back and get paid.** The company that pays them (the joint venture business partner we're aligned with) has been in business now for over 10 years, and they've already paid out close to two *billion* dollars to their affiliates. By the time you read this, they will have broken that two billion dollar mark—so they are very solid.

This Health Resource Portal is going to contain all kinds of articles, too; ultimately, hundreds of alternative health experts are going to write articles and share stories, and we're going to interview some of them, and post the interviews in both audio and video. **This is going to be exciting!** It's a big, bold, brassy move on our part, and we're trying to get it all ready to go for our big kick-off that's coming up very soon. We've got a cut-off date; and as that cut-off date approaches, the pressure is on, and we're feeling that pressure!

For our customers it's a big, bold idea and it's going to get them excited. **It's new. It's different. It's interesting. It's got huge value. Our offer gives them all this tremendous value for the lowest possible price—a price that's just going to blow their minds!** But from our perspective, because it's new and because there are so many different things that we're trying to accomplish and because we've got a firm deadline, it's somewhat nerve-wracking. The pressure is on! We want to make a great presentation and we've got dates set, so there definitely is some fear involved—though we are confident we can do it.

It's all about making huge promises—big, bold promises that get your prospects and clients excited. You're looking for the things that will make them want to stand in line with money in hand and beg you to take it—things that are going to captivate their imaginations, things that are going to make them salivate with greed. You want them to want it so bad they can barely contain themselves. **To get there, you have to make bigger and bigger and bigger promises, the kind you know the people in your marketplace want the most.** You need to captivate their imaginations and get them very excited.

Part of the secret here is making promises that you're not sure exactly how you're going to fulfill. Sure, that's a little scary—and the idea frightens some marketers out of the market, because there's no way that they would ever step outside their comfort zones. **But how can you succeed without risk?** Take some chances. **Step out in faith, deal with the fear, and let the energy from the fear and the pressure from the deadlines drive you.** Let it all just percolate, forcing you to come up with ideas as you go along. **I promise you that if you do this, you'll invent things you never would have if you had taken the safe, conservative approach.** If you just waited until you had everything figured out and you knew exactly how it was all going to go down, there'd be no pressure to perform, sure; but there'd be none of the big, bold, brassy kinds of promises required to really captivate people.

Today's marketplace is overcrowded. I'm not pointing this

out for negative reasons; this is just reality. **The consumer has more choices than ever before.** Now, some of the marketers in this overcrowded marketplace are razor sharp—they're very aggressive, and they're out there doing all kinds of crazy things to get people's attention. **They understand that the customer only has so much disposable income, and so you have to constantly push it as far as you can in order to get that money.** That means making the biggest, boldest promises possible, the kind that give the potential buyer the benefits that you *know* they'll go crazy over. **You have to push it, push it, and push it even more in order to stay competitive.** This forces you to deal with lots of uncertainty and fear—things that might scare other people to death.

Fear is a funny thing. It doesn't have to immobilize you. Consider roller coasters. On the really dangerous ones, some people practically pass out, because their minds just can't take all the ups and downs and the pure fear that results. And yet, it's also exciting! You can easily see that fear is excitement in a carnival ride or a horror movie, where you know what outcome to expect—or at least you feel that you're going to make it. When we were in Branson last summer, we all went riding on these zip lines, and there was this one tower that you jumped off of that was 120 feet off the ground. It was a free-fall drop they'd once used to train parachute jumpers. So you jump off this 120-foot tower, and you're in free fall for a while; and then, in the last 30 feet or so the line starts to tighten. By the time you hit the ground, you're basically at rest. There's somebody down there to help you, too. It's sort of like jumping out of an airplane, except that you have a thin wire strapped onto a little harness on your back. Well, some people have stood up on that tower, they told us, for up to six hours in total fear... Because once you get up on the tower, you can't easily get down any other way. You have to take a zip line over to the tower in the first place.

Now, they probably *could* get you down some other way, but it wouldn't be easy. That's why they've had people who just stood on that tower for hours before they finally decided to jump. Well it didn't take me six hours! **I stood up there for about 10 minutes, and then I was ready.** I was right there on the edge; I was looking down at the drop, and then all of a sudden the guy in charge says, "Now, don't jump!" And I said, "What do you mean, don't jump?"

I was ready to do it. I had psyched myself up. **And he replies, "Just walk off the platform."**

Well, that was even scarier. All of a sudden my knees buckled, and I actually just sort of fell off! It scared the crap out of me—and I was scared for about two hours afterwards. My whole nervous system was shaken up! **But I did it because I knew it *would* scare me, and I knew that I had to confront my fears.** Lots of people do things like that because they know it's good for them, and they know that it's going to help them feel a little better about themselves. It helps them conquer fear.

Look, the more you shirk this, the more you pull back, the weaker you become. **And the weaker you become, the more your fears control you.** That's the irony of it all. People who have a lot of fears—who hold back because of those fears— usually find that their fears multiply, and pretty soon the fear has completely taken over. They're afraid of everything. So you've got to learn how to make a break from it. **Even in the** marketing world, and the moneymaking world, you have to do things that scare you. You have to stretch yourself. You have to force yourself. You have to make promises you have only a vague idea of how to keep. **You have to take a leap of faith, and be willing to just put it all out there.** It's frightening, but it's also invigorating. Just like those carnival rides, just like the horror movies, it's fun… it's exciting!

Fear and excitement are the same emotion, viewed from different perspectives. When you're fearful, you're thinking everything is going to go wrong—and you end up freaking out. When you look at it as excitement, you realize that there may be some danger to it, like when I jumped off that 120-foot tower. I knew there was a possibility that the harness might break. But I still felt like I was fairly safe.

You have to make fear your friend. If something doesn't scare you, don't do it. So many businesspeople just want to follow the safe path. All they want to do is work on small ideas that are doable. They just want to keep doing the same thing over and over. The customers get bored, the sales and profits go flat, and in the end they suffer. Don't be a part of that group.

Choose new, exciting ventures to invest your time, money, effort, and energy in. **If it's not going to stretch you, then pass it by. And realize that if you're actively seeking such opportunities, the ideas for them will abound.** We encounter people occasionally who tell us, "You guys come up with ideas all the time, but I don't know how to get ideas." The truth is, we have so many ideas and so little time that we have to be really choosy about the ideas we do pursue. **If people knew how many ideas we discarded, they might be shocked!** Because when you're in that mindset of looking for opportunities for new ventures, they're all over the place. **Then it comes down to choosing the few you actually want to pursue.** The best ones always induce some risk and some fear. I think that you have to continue to stretch yourself in that way—so things don't get boring. If an opportunity isn't a little challenging, then you should probably avoid it.

There are two different directions from which you might enter this scenario. In the first, you're not successful yet; so you're looking for any and every deal you can find, because nothing is working so far. The other scenario would be that you're already a successful entrepreneur. You've got several deals going, and you're just looking for something that's new, different, and exciting, the next big thing you're going to invest your time, money and energy in. **Either way, you need to find things that challenge you and push you beyond what you're comfortable doing.**

Most people had a tendency to skew their decisions toward comfort and ease. In business, that means we end up looking for ventures that offer as little risk as possible, where there's not a whole lot of money or time required of us. We play it safe... which means we tend toward mediocrity. **But by avoiding the risk, we also avoid any potential for reward.** We like to dabble in things, in part so that when they don't work out as we hoped, we can always say, "Well, I was just dabbling." It's sort of like someone who plays the stock market part-time. They put a little money into the effort and they buy and sell stocks here and there, but they never go all in. They're hoping they at least break even and don't lose much money—but they're never out there putting it all on the line, hoping for a big gain.

That's not to equate investing with gambling—although some of the characteristics are similar. However, you certainly take on risk when you make any type of investment, including opening a business. **It's axiomatic that the opportunities that require the most risk, or that require the greatest stretching of your mind and abilities, are usually the ones that produce the greatest potential rewards.** So as an investor, you have to decide where you want to come down on that line.

You can say, "I want to minimize my risk as much as possible," and usually that means something like putting your money into a money market account. The government insures your money up to $100,000, and you get a guaranteed half-percent interest. It's not a particularly wise investment strategy, but it's certainly an ultra-safe bet. On the other end of the spectrum, you could go the extreme risk route, investing in all kinds of emerging technologies that haven't proven themselves. When you do that, you know going in that some of these companies aren't going to be around a couple of years from now, but you're hoping something works, because such deals have the potential for huge rewards. But they're also extremely risky.

Most people fall somewhere in the middle of the spectrum, whether with personal investments or business strategies. Where you fall on that line will determine your potential for reward or for financial gain as a result of your entrepreneurial decisions.

I contend that you should err on the side of the "stretch" whenever possible. Err on the side of doing things that require putting yourself out there; things that scare you a bit, though in the good way that a roller coaster does. You're looking for things that put you on the edge of your seat as you anticipate the results, knowing that the money and energy you've put into it may very well pay off big for you.

Here's an example from Chris Lakey's life. It's not business-related *per se*, but I think it's apropos. Chris and his wife are working with a few other folks to start a foster home for orphans in China. They're negotiating with a company out in California that they hope will provide the financial support. That company already has a 501(c)(3) tax exemption status, so they've got their legal non-profit structure in place; if everything goes right, this will make it tremendously easier for Chris and his wife and friends to raise the funds they need. Chris's group is casting a big vision for what they think this venture could be; they've developed a Mission Statement, and they're pushing for something very bold and daring.

They're not looking for financial gain here, so in the business sense, we're not talking about risk/reward for profit. **But there *is* both risk and reward, in the sense that this is a big project.** It's no less a risk than any entrepreneurial project, given the project's international scope. Chris and his group have big ideas for it, because their goal is to generate massive action to help orphans in China. In working toward that, they've shared their plan with the Board of this non-profit they're hoping to partner with.

Chris says that he doesn't think, at this point, that the Board sees their big vision yet. No doubt they're looking at it as a risky situation, and they want Chris and his group to slow down, to take baby steps into the project—which is probably the prudent way to go. And of course, the potential backers are putting their non-profit status on the line, so Chris's group has to do things by their book if they want the Board's help. **Chris and his group agree with some of the Board's ideas, but they're still going back and forth between the big vision, which is pretty scary and definitely has risks, versus the non-profit's desire to play it safer.**

If you want a big reward in anything, you have to take risks. **If you're a businessperson and you're planning to do things in a low-key way, if you're going to play it safe... then why do it at all?** Ask yourself what your goals are, what you're trying to accomplish, and then look at your model. If you're not being stretched, if you're not a little bit scared about this new venture—if it doesn't induce some risk on your part—then ask yourself why you should even bother? What are you hoping to get out of it?

I think you'll find that putting yourself out there on a regular basis is more fulfilling than holding back. I'm not saying that going all-in is always the best decision, but some people do mortgage it all when they find something to really believe in. They put it all on the line, not just moneywise but reputation-wise sometimes, to make their business dreams a reality. And if that doesn't scare you, I don't know what will! That's why they say it's usually best to get into these kinds of things when you're young and dumb. The older we get, the more conservative and set in our ways we tend to become. Well, it doesn't matter how old you are, and it doesn't matter what life stage you're at; this principle still applies. If you're looking for business success you have to stretch yourself, you have to scare yourself, and you have to put yourself at risk. **Without those things, the potential for reward usually doesn't exist. And without the potential for reward, there's no real reason to get in business...** so you should probably look elsewhere for entertainment value, or whatever other goal you're aiming for.

Too many people try to take the safe approach. They think they're being smart by trying to plan everything precisely, but they fail to appreciate all the market forces at work against them. Military planners know that no battle plan survives contact with the enemy—and in a broader sense, no business plan survives contact with reality, unless it's very flexible. And ultimately, it's all about the consumer. The consumer has more choices today than ever before, and only so much disposable income. **Playing it safe just isn't going to work, because there are too many other marketers and companies and individuals out there who *aren't* playing it safe.** If you're not careful, they're going to end up getting all the money, not you.

So a word to the wise: if you're a naturally conservative person, partner up with people who aren't. Which leads us quite naturally to our

🐛🐛🐛🐛🐛

CHAPTER TEN

Take good care of the people who take good care of you!

🐛🐛🐛

Take Good Care of the People Who Take Care of You

If somebody's taking good care of you, then you'd better take good care of them. **That's just common sense...** or so you might think. And yet, if it really *was* common sense, everybody would be doing it... and they're not.

Business people lose sight of this point surprisingly often.

It's my fundamental belief that nobody ever gets rich by themselves. It always takes the combined efforts of a group of people with complementary skills and abilities. So find the very best people that you possibly can—smart, talented people you can trust—whose skills and talents balance your own. You can't just match skill sets one-to-one. **What matters is the synergistic effort of a group of people who have different backgrounds and abilities, who all come together that create something that's greater than the sum of the individual parts.**

My favorite analogy here is the old-fashioned clock or watch. I love those antique timepieces. You pull the back off, and you see all these tiny gears nested together. It's an engineering marvel, really. In my analogy, each one of those gears represents either a person or, if the company's big enough, a department. All the gears work together to make the timepiece run smoothly and accurately—and they're all necessary to ensure proper function. The same is true in a business. **You need everyone working together, contributing**

their own talents, to make it work correctly. If you study the most powerful and profitable companies, you'll see that it's never the entrepreneur up front—the one who gets all the attention—that really matters. **It's the combined, synergistic effort of a group that drives the company's success. That's why when you find the right people, you need to hold onto them and you take good care of them.**

Now, this is something that I've worked hard on. Getting along with people and working smoothly with them is not my strong suit. I *try* to do it Sometimes, the best way for me to get along with people is to just leave them alone most of the time; less is more. I try to find good people and let them do their thing so I can do *my* thing. The less involvement they have with me, sometimes, the better. Back when I was first getting started 30 years ago, I knew intuitively that this was the way to go. **Even though I was just in my early 20s, I knew that I wasn't going to make it on my own. I knew that I needed other people. I** simply hadn't been blessed with all the talents and abilities I needed to make it big. Maybe the fact that I accepted that is the reason that I *did* make it.

I realize that this concept is simplistic and doesn't apply to all situations, but I think it's applicable to most. Furthermore, I think that one of the reasons why some entrepreneurs don't make it is that people who really *are* skilled in a lot of different areas don't need any help. They can do it all on their own... and this damages them, in the end. I wasn't that way. I needed help, and I knew I needed help. Although I was young and dumb and had a lot of learning to do (still am... still do!), I knew I wasn't going to make it on my own. **So I went through a couple of**

business partnerships before I met Eileen, who became my third and final business partner... as well as my wife and best friend.

When I first went into business for myself, I was a salesman. I could go knock on doors all day long, I could call up people all day long, and I didn't care if people slammed doors in my face. I was a hustler, a pitchman—and my first two business partners were just like me. But Eileen's not a salesperson. She's very analytical, pragmatic, a behind-the-scenes type. She has loads of common sense, lots of wisdom, and skills complementary to mine. **So it's not too general a statement to say that my first two partnerships went sour because two people were doing the same job. When Eileen became my business partner, we formed an excellent team.**

And that's all this is really about: teamwork. Here's a simple quote from John Wooden, the college basketball coach who won more games than any other coach in history: "I don't want my five best players on the court. I want my best five." This is a word play that works at a conceptual level. You see, in basketball there are five players on the court per team. But Wooden didn't just want to throw five great players out on the boards. He wanted to have his best *team* out there—in other words, the five best players who played the best together. That concept sticks in your head, and it says everything to me. We all know that there are players who have enormous talent, but don't play well with others. **He wanted his best five, the five who, together as a unit, as a team, could create that synergistic force that leads to greatness.**

When you have something like that in sports, all of a

sudden you become elevated. You become the best there is. It's one of the reasons I love football so much. There are 11 players per team out there on the field. Just try to get 11 people moving in one direction. Try to get 11 people to agree on *anything*, especially when they have to constantly change their strategy. It's poetry in motion when it works well—when you watch a truly awesome team that blends perfectly. **The same thing is true in business. When you have a group of people who work together in a synergistic way, it's a pleasure to see them in operation—and it's profitable to experience, in all senses of the word.**

Let me repeat: in the ideal business team, the individual members have complementary skills and abilities. They're not all the same, whether in their actions or experiences or in their ways of thinking; but they're all smart, at the tops of their respective games. They take their work seriously; they're in it to win, and they're in it with all their hearts. **When this happens, a magical situation is created, and you're on your way to making millions of dollars.** I'm not exaggerating about that!

So in the final analysis, it's not the entrepreneur up front who matters; it's the people behind the scenes who work smoothly together to create a unique, profitable corporate culture.

Recently, I read Walter Isaacson's brilliant book *Steve Jobs,* which came out right after Jobs died. As you know, Jobs was the front man for Apple Computers (which is now simply called "Apple"). **But behind the scenes, he worked with a tight group of people with extraordinary skills and abilities**

complimentary to his own. Their hearts were in it all the way. They were as deeply committed as he was… to the point where they slept it, they ate it, they breathed it. **The job was part of them—not just something they did to pay the bills. They did it out of a sense of total pride.**

In every rags-to-riches story, there are people behind the scenes who supported and uplifted the hero. This is especially true in business. **When you find those people in your organization, take very, very good care of them.** Make sure they have the skills you need, and make sure they're people you can trust. **The smarter they are and the more skills they have, the more you can just let them do what they do while you try to focus on whatever makes the most money for the company.** Do it right, and you can sit back and watch the money just flow in. It really can be that simple. Now, that doesn't mean it's *easy*. In fact, the more you're stretching yourself, the harder it is. But the principle truly is that simple.

There's an old saying that applies here: "You scratch my back, I'll scratch yours." **In life, we tend to take care of our people; people we know, people who are close to us, people we care about.** That's not to say we don't take care of other people we *don't* know; America is one of the most charitable nations on the planet. But in a relationship sense, we tend to help the people who are closest to us first. So assuming we're on good terms with our families, and assuming we have relationships with friends, we do things for them. When they need help moving, we go rent a U-Haul and load it up with stuff and help them move. If they need something we can spare, we help them out. We provide any assistance we can. That's just what we do with people we care about.

We all recognize that—and it's the same way in business. **You build relationships with other people, including suppliers or vendors.** In our business, we send out a massive amount of mail, so we have a strong relationship with our printer. We also have significant relationships with a mailing house, mailing list brokers, and other people who are important to our business model. Now, in *your* business model, you may have different kinds of relationships. If you have a restaurant, you might be close to the food suppliers and paper vendors, as well as those who supply décor, utensils, etc. If you have a retail shop, you'll have your own set of suppliers and vendors.

Depending on what kind of business you have, you have different people in and around your business on whom you rely, people you've (ideally) built good relationships with. **There's a certain level of trust there. These people do things for you, and in turn you want to do things for them. You watch out for them.** In the case of a good supplier, you refer people to them. In the case of friends in the business who serve the same marketplace, you look for opportunities to joint venture; that is, you provide them with opportunities to do business with some of your customers, and they provide you with opportunities to do business with some of theirs. **In short, you have to take care of people and hope that they return the favor. In most good business relationships, that happens naturally.**

Now, this process can go bad, especially when public money is involved. People get upset when they hear about "no bid" contracts being given to political donors, for example, but it happens regularly. So here you have someone in Congress (or sometimes even higher office) who rewards their donors—some of which are big companies—when they get elected, because those donors expect some special consideration as a result. "You scratch my back and I'll scratch yours... I helped get you elected, so now I'm expecting you to send some government contracts my way, or do things that benefit my industry." **It's bad enough that public taxpayer money is involved; but political favors can also breed conflicts of interest. That's obviously a bad idea, and most people can see that.**

In all other aspects of life, though, it's a *good* idea to cut mutually beneficial deals with the people you're closest to. Personal life is full of opportunities like that, and business should be as well. When you take good care of people who take good care of you, you're just setting up your relationship to benefit both parties. That's really what it's all about, and it happens across a lot of industries. I see no reason not to arrange such things within your own circle of influence—that is, all the people you encounter and work with on an ongoing basis. For example, your employees (if you have any); your co-workers, if you work for somebody else; family members and business partners and joint venture partners and suppliers—everybody you work with on a regular basis. That's your circle of influence. You might call this your "wedding and funeral list," and maybe it would be even bigger than that.

It all comes down to being kind to people and doing things that are in their best interests. **In business, it just means letting people know that you care about them, and letting them know that you're there for them—that you have their back.**

Hopefully, they would do the same for you.

That's the way it is with our suppliers. **We're always looking to refer new customers to the people we do business with.** If we have a good relationship with a vendor and their product category comes up in conversation with someone else, we recommend them. We're always telling people things like, "Here's our list broker. If you're looking to get into the mail order business and want to rent the same kinds of lists we work with, here's who you should contact." Or, "If you need a good printer, here's who you should use." "If you need a good Internet host, here's who you can use for that."

Recently, our printer told us about somebody he does business with whom he thought *we* should be doing business with—so the practice goes both ways. That raises everybody up. We're looking for opportunities to help them make more money in their businesses, and they're looking for opportunities to help us to make more money in *our* business and, in the end, everybody wins and is better for it.

Some people call this process "enlightened selfishness," which I think is a delightful term. I'm completely on the other end of the spectrum from those who think that selfishness is a terrible thing. Come on, now. We *all* care about ourselves; that's just the way it is. It's a survival mechanism, rooted into us at a cellular level. Can we overcome it? Of course we can, in the best of times. On a day-to-day basis, however, we're all looking out for Number One. **But "enlightened selfishness" is where you're also looking out for other people... not just for their benefit, but for your own.**

By taking good care of the people who take good care of you, you're also taking better care of *you*.

Contrast this approach with all those egotistical monsters out there. Most entrepreneurs are egotistical to some extent, but a few take it to extremes. They can't get along with anybody, they can't work with anybody, they don't value other people, they only think of themselves. Whenever they *do* try to reach out to other people, their actions come across as extremely manipulative. You can't trust them. You ask yourself, "If I was really in a pinch and I didn't have something that they wanted, would they help me?" The answer, most often, is no. There are plenty of people like that, and they'll never be able to pull together a team of people and work within that team to do anything on a grand scale.

But if you really want to make millions of dollars, and keep and build those millions, that's what you've got to do! You don't have any other choice. **You've got to find a group of people who have your back, while you have theirs. They need to know they can count on you when the chips are down.** They need to know that if it happened to be four o'clock in the morning and they were in deep, deep trouble, they could call you and you'd be there for them (even though you might be a little ticked off at first!). And vice versa.

By taking care of people who take good care of you, you're also taking good care of yourself. That's enlightened selfishness in a nutshell, and they ought to be teaching it in Kindergarten. That's how commonsensical it is.

Of course, so many of the things I discuss in this book

135

sound like common sense... and yet so many people violate these principals every single day. **It's all about money to them, and ultimately, that's their downfall.** There's no loyalty to suppliers, staff, or customers. They're not looking out for others in any way. At the first sign of trouble, they're gone.

That takes place all too often in Internet marketing these days—and this is one of my biggest pet peeves. Most Internet marketers just want to sit at home and tap around on the computer all day. They want their relationships to be email-based; they never want to meet people face-to-face. **They never want to invest any real time with those people. It's all superficial at best, which is not the best foundation to build substantial relationships on.** In relationships like that, people know that you *don't* have their backs and that they really can't trust you. Well, that's just not going to fly.

I don't want to come across as self-righteous here. I've made plenty of mistakes in my time, and I've let people down time and again. But I believe I've learned from those mistakes. The people I work with all know how much I care about them—how much I value them. **That's the *only* way to build lasting relationships: to honestly care about the people you deal with every day, from employees to coworkers, suppliers to customers.**

CHAPTER ELEVEN

Put your entire focus on making a BIGGER PIE — not on counting and weighing each slice!

Focus on Making a Bigger Pie

In business, you need to put your entire focus on creating a bigger pie, *not* on counting and weighing each slice of the existing pie.

As I've told you before, **it's all about thinking *bigger*.** You don't have to look at that metaphorical pie and assume that just because it's a certain size now, that's as big as it's ever going to get. So many people miss the point here; they want to carefully analyze everything, based on assumptions that aren't always warranted. They're looking at the business from the wrong end. **What you need to do instead is set some huge goals—get a vision for what you want to do—and move forward on faith, not worrying too much about the details.** You can take care of those as you encounter them.

We're starting a brand new business, and one of our goals is to bring in one billion dollars in our first 15 years. Now, that's a lot of money—but it's also a long vision. Within the first few years we hope to get close to the $100 million mark, so it's not like we're going to wait until the last five years to make the bulk of our money. **We call our business plan "The $100-Million A Year Business Plan," because that's our target goal.**

Needless to say, just having a plan or a vision for what you want to accomplish isn't a guarantee in any way—but it's a

start. It sets you up to succeed, and of course when you go to the bank or try to get people to invest with you, they'll want a good, solid business plan. Ideally, they want a very clear vision, where you're thinking big and have everything spelled out, every "i" dotted and every "t" crossed—where you've thought it all through. There's no way you're going to get people involved without that.

With the *right* business plan, with big enough goals, if you're involved in a big enough marketplace where other people are generating massive amounts of money doing things that are fairly similar to what you want to do, you're golden. **Although, of course, you do have to try to come up with something unique; you need to look for gaps in the marketplace, unfulfilled areas or points of differentiation that separate you from what everybody else is doing.** All that is vitally important. **And yet, the basic marketplace is, well, basic.** If others are doing what you want to do in a general way, and if they're bringing in millions every year, there's no reason why you can't bring in millions too.

We're starting our new business, based on our "$100-Million A Year Business Plan," because there are companies already in this market that are doing similar things and profiting to the tune of a *billion* dollars per year—although we've got something totally unique. **I'm confident that if they can do it, we can do it—and the same thing goes for you. That has to be your business mantra, your vision, and it has to fill your heart.** You can't just believe in it; it must be so fundamental that it's beyond belief, into the realm of total certainty. I don't know if we even have words for that in English; but the point is, it has to be something that's ingrained in you.

Look, **it takes no more work to think big than it does to think small.** So many people are afraid to do it, though, so they're always holding back. They don't want to lose their money. They don't want to look like fools or be embarrassed, or end up being one of the wild-eyed dreamers who fails so spectacularly that they go down in history. So they hold back; and in so doing, they think they're being smart. In some ways, they are; you can't argue that. But when you look at the business through the wrong end of the scope, and you careful analyze and weigh out everything little thing before you take a step... well, you know what? **It's not going to matter much in the end. You're going to get blindsided along the way not matter what. I promise you that. Contingency planning is necessary, but it only takes you so far.**

You have to figure things out as you go. If you think big and head toward that huge goal, it helps you cross the bridges as you come to them, and deal with the associated problems. You've got a flexibility that obsessive perfectionists lack. If you've ever spent much time in the self-development world, you probably already know this quote: *The "why" to do something is far more important than "how" you're actually going to accomplish it.* I've used it myself in this book. But knowing something and internalizing it are two entirely different things.

If you study the lives of entrepreneurs who started with nothing and turned that into something very substantial, you'll see that they gambled big along the way. **Inevitably, there were all kinds of little failures and sometimes even big failures in their lives.** Thomas Edison, for example: his first thousand attempts to invent the light bulb failed... but then he succeeded in a big way. People like Edison keep on believing in themselves, keep on believing in their visions, and keep on thinking bigger than other people do! **They don't let all the distractions and failures stop them.**

They aren't held back by fear. Instead of thinking about what everything's going to cost, as fiscal conservatives so often do, entrepreneurial visionaries think about how much money they can *make* by expand_ng their vision. When you do that, you take that same mental energy and put it not into worrying about the obstacles, but in framing the outcome. **You should be putting your real focus on trying to make as much money as you can, instead of counting pennies and overthinking every little detail.** You can hire people to handle those details when and if they come up.

You know, everybody likes to hear about our rags-to-riches success here at M.O.R.E., Inc.; they enjoy hearing about the millions of dollars we've made. People love that story about all the years we struggled, and all that we went through. But I'll be the first to admit that often, those times weren't all that pleasant. In some ways, our life was a living hell... but we did keep believing in ourselves, and we finally made our millions. All that is true. In our first five years in business, we generated over ten million dollars; then we went on to generate over one hundred million dollars in total revenue within our first 19 years. All that happened after we were poor for a number of years, and struggled along while our friends and family laughed at us.

Those are the stories that people want to hear. What they *don't* want to hear are the parts that we rarely ever tell... but I'll give you a little peek of that now. Most people don't want to hear that there's been a lot of confusion, frustration, and heartbreak along the way. **There were many times when we just thought about giving up**—a lot of times when we questioned ourselves and said, "Oh my God, why did we even *do* this?" **There have been times when we've lost tons of money and things haven't worked out;** times when we've been moving in five different directions, and then suddenly had to cut it back to two or one. And there have been plenty of times when I've just moved in too many wrong directions at once, times when I've done things too impulsively, without thinking things through enough in the very beginning. **I often advise you not to overanalyze, as I did earlier, but you should analyze *some*!**

We've experienced quite a bit of failure along the way. But we've had more successes than failures, and we keep moving forward. On average, everything has worked out phenomenally well for us!

I'm involved in a business right now that's about 18 months old. It's been a struggle from the very beginning; we're undercapitalized. The sales have gone up and down; looking at the sales graph is like looking at the blueprints for a roller coaster. Now, if you take all of those ups and downs and put a line through the whole thing to determine the general direction, you'll see that each month is better than the previous one, and we're consistently making more money. But if you look at it on a daily basis, or focus on the slow weeks, you might think, "God, this is a nightmare! We're never going to make it!" But I've learned that you just have to keep having faith in yourself. **If you keep believing those big dreams, and you stay**

with the game, you'll ultimately come out ahead.

So many entrepreneurs think way too small. Their
business ideas are too small. **The markets they're trying to
serve are often tiny niche markets, which are always going to
make them tiny amounts of money.** That's fine if that's what
you want; if that's your dream, if that's your vision for your life, if
that's what's making you happy… then go for it. But if that's *not*
what you want—if you want your day in the sun, or a bigger piece
of a bigger pie, then you've got to do what I'm suggesting. If you
want to see how far you can go, how high you can fly, and what's
possible for you, you've got to set those bigger goals. **You've got
to focus on baking that bigger pie instead of counting and
weighing each slice of a smaller one you've settled for.**

Think about it as a Million Dollar Parade. You're out
there, going for the million-dollar prize—or even the billion-
dollar one. Let's say you're moving forward, trying to make a
lot of money... and you look down and you see a bunch of $100
bills lying on the ground. Well, you don't have time to stop to
pick those up! Walk right over them. Let all the people *behind
you* waste their time picking up those little $100 bills. **You're
not here to make $100 at a time; you're out to make millions
of dollars.** *That* should be your focus!

**To go back to the pie analogy, which is one so many
people use, I think that too often we limit ourselves by
thinking about the money universe as a pie of finite size.** That
causes us to minimize our dreams about what it's possible to do
in the marketplace. But it doesn't have to be this way, because
economic "pies" can scale up and down. A quick example: as I'm

writing this, our government is pretty much broke, and there's a lot of discussion about what to do about it—although there aren't many people willing to talk about actually cutting the size of our government pie. But you do hear a lot of people talking about the amount of money that's in our economy. Some people might contend that this group or that one isn't getting their fair share, or that this agency needs this much of the pie, or that this industry makes obscene profits and that somehow means another industry must be struggling. They tie our economy together in one big monolithic pie that consists of a fixed, invariable dollar amount. But the size of the national economic "pie" is *not* fixed. It can grow or shrink, based on a number of factors. Some of the reasons it changes are behavioral; some have broader causes. **The money supply ebbs and flows, so the pie is sometimes quite large, and sometimes it's smaller.**

This also applies on a much smaller scale, from individual companies and portfolios down to the decisions that people make on a personal level. **So the strategy here should be focused on building a bigger pie instead of micro-managing the pie you have access to.** Don't limit yourself by thinking that there's only so many people you can serve in a potential marketplace, and believing you can only extract a certain amount of income from that marketplace each year. **Instead, work to increase your market share; or expand to a larger market.** Don't just blindly accept what you see as all there can ever be. That kind of thinking throttles your ability to innovate and grow.

Let's say you have a $100,000 pie, and you perceive it as breaking down to five $20,000 pieces. If you take the old limited view and want to grow any slice of the pie, another slice has to shrink. But what happens when you double the size of the overall pie to $200,000? **Instantly, the value of each slice doubles; although each piece still represents a set percentage of the whole, you've grown the pie, so each slice is bigger in absolute terms.**

Those are really your only two options for growth of a particular slice. You either borrow (or steal) money from one of the other slices, or you make the pie itself bigger. Period. **I think the better option is self-evident: rather than starve one important slice in favor of another, grow the whole pie.** Barring a few economic factors and, yes, basic business cycles and the occasional bad month, there's no reason you shouldn't be able to grow your economic pie if you're willing to be aggressive enough in promoting your business—as you must be, if you intend to survive.

Let's look at this from another angle. Sometimes, as I discussed earlier, how you promote your business is impacted by how big a total pie you feel like there is in your marketplace. Again, this is somewhat limiting. Let's say there's a specific share of money spent on fast food in your town. If you own one of those fast food joints, you're getting a portion of the town's fast food pie. Suppose that amounts to $10,000 per day, and there are 10 fast food restaurants in your town (we're using nice, round numbers to make it easy to conceptualize). Well, if everything's equal, then each fast food restaurant gets 10% of that fast food pie—$1,000 per day.

If an eleventh fast food restaurant comes to town, it's going to shake things up. In the traditional scenario, it's going to eat away at somebody's (or everybody's) share of that $10,000 pie; to make everything equal (which never actually happens), they'll have to split the pie into 11 pieces now, and everyone suffers. Well, that's *one* scenario. Another scenario is that the new fast food restaurant comes into town and the owner says, "We think there's more room for growth, so we're going to promote fast food to the marketplace of this city." Let's say they do a good job of it, and the resulting rising tide lifts all boats. Suddenly, instead of $10,000 a day being spent on fast food, they might increase that pie to $15,000 daily. That's another effective way to increase the amount of money they make, even if they don't increase the size of their slice of the pie. Ideally, they'd want to get the entire increase for themselves, and leave the $1,000 per day to all the other restaurants; **but whatever happens, they want the pie to grow so they can carve out a bigger niche for themselves within that marketplace.**

Both your marketplace pie, and the size of the slice you claim, will shrink or grow based on how successful you are at doing business. Don't be afraid to go all out and build a bigger pie, because you benefit both yourself and your community—and the bigger the pie you can create, the more important things you can do for yourself and others. Divide the slices as you will, but make that pie as large as you want to, and as large as your marketplace will bear—which in most cases is a *lot* larger than it is right now.

So think BIG, and build a bigger pie! Don't worry about counting and weighing each slice. That's just another way of limiting yourself.

CHAPTER TWELVE

All growth comes from consciously living outside of your comfort zone.

If you're not doing things on a regular basis that scare you just a little (or a lot!) — you're not growing.

All Growth Comes From Consciously Living Outside Of Your Comfort Zone

If you're not doing things on a regular basis that scare you a little, or a lot, then you're not growing. You don't want to end up on your deathbed filled with regrets, saying, "I wish I could have gone for it. I wish I had done more." **You want to live your life unfiltered. Go for it! Pace yourself, but also push yourself very hard.**

All growth occurs outside of your comfort zone. Being too comfortable can be a bad thing. First of all, it's boring. **Second, it means you're never going to develop yourself in the fullest possible way.** That's why you've got to keep the pressure on. You've got to always have more in the air than you can comfortably handle. **You've got to live with fear and frustration and confusion, and make those things your constant traveling companions.** It's all right to feel those things sometimes, because it means you're alive and moving forward.

There's a person who works for our company who used to tell me, "Take it easy!" But every time he'd say it, I'd get in his face and reply, "I don't *want* to take it easy! I'll take it easy when I'm dead! I've got eternity to take it easy!" **Right now, you see, I want to live full out. I want to go for it. I want to experience everything, good and bad.** So many people think they can hide out from life, avoiding all kinds of problems and pain; but in the end the joke is on them, because they never develop the kinds of talents, skills, and abilities they need to really succeed. **You can only develop those when you're *not* taking it easy**—when you push yourself constantly, asking and demanding more of yourself. That's how you become everything you're capable of becoming.

Set bigger goals; that's a lot of it right there. When you do that, and then start moving forward in the direction of your dreams, you box yourself in, forcing yourself to succeed. **Make commitments that you don't know how you're going to fulfill, exactly.** Make big, bold promises—and then figure out how you're going to overcome all the obstacles in the way. Admittedly, by doing this you can get yourself in trouble sometimes—and because you're constantly stretching yourself, it's not always fun, and it doesn't always feel good. **Yet, a big part of discipline is learning that things that are good for you don't have to *feel* good.** Things can feel really, really bad sometimes, and they certainly do when you're living with the emotional and mental anguish that you have to live with sometimes when you're pushing yourself and demanding more out of life.

It's sort of like going to the gym. If you want to build a great body, you're going to have to work out regularly. You're going to have to push yourself, sweat, and endure some aches and pains along the way. We all know that! Those great bodies don't happen by accident. **They happen because people have a vision for themselves.** They decide they want to get strong or buff. They first set that vision, and then they go in the gym and live there for up to 3-5 hours a day.

Business can be the same way. I know for a fact—since I'm living proof—that anybody in American can get rich. Despite a lot of whining out there, on the part of a lot of people who claim that we just don't have any real freedoms, the bottom line is that you're as free as you want to be. **You create your own economy.** And yes, there are external forces beyond your control, but what it boils down to is what the old quote tells you: "If it's meant to be, it's up to me." Anybody in America can get rich. Yes, I know the government keeps getting bigger. Yes, it interferes with our lives. And yes, taxes keep going up. Blah, blah, blah… go sing it to somebody else! **I don't have time to focus on all that negativity. I'm trying to live my dreams, and I'm trying to think big, and I'm trying to move forward, and so are plenty of other entrepreneurs—and you should be, too.** If you want to make a lot of money, you *can* make a lot of money. But making excuses and making big money are mutually exclusive, folks.

You can't make excuses and whine and cry about how bad the world is, and how everybody is out to get you, and how nothing ever goes your way. It doesn't matter whether you think it's true or not—it won't fly, and people don't want to hear it. **Instead, go out there and make an effort. Do big things, bold things that you think will make a lot of money.** You see, people who are great at making excuses never succeed as much as they might otherwise, because they're wasting their time and energy on those excuses, and convincing themselves to hold back. As a result, they never push themselves hard enough and they never reach their fullest potential. Their excuses become their chains… and ultimately, the reasons why they decide they're just going to take it easy.

THINK BIGGER!

This is just part of the human condition, and we can't escape it fully. We all have the need for comfort and security, and we like our pleasure. We like total certainty. **We like for things to be easy. Too often, people want to live fully in their comfort zones.** They want everything to be easy and smooth; they want all the benefits of hard work without having to push themselves, without constantly demanding more. This makes them soft in every way a person can become soft.

So if you really want to succeed, push yourself very hard most of the time—but be sure to pace yourself. There's this misconception that says that stress is a bad thing. It's not; to some extent, stress is healthy and necessary. What's bad is strain: too much stress unbroken by periods of relaxation. That's what wears you down. So do pace yourself. Have a routine. **Have times of the day when things are quiet, times when you're working very intensely, and times when you're kicking back and doing things you enjoy.**

The few skills I've developed over the years (and they're too few, in my view) were as a result of pushing myself well beyond my comfort zone. For example: from the first time I saw Russ von Hoelscher write sales letters, I wanted to write like he did. We'd hire him for the weekend; he'd fly out to Wichita, we'd bring him home to Goessel, and he'd spend the weekend writing sales letters for us. Then he would fly back to El Cajon, California. We would take those sales letters he wrote out by hand, have our typist type them, and then we'd mail them out to our customers... and the money would just roll in!

Eileen and I would brainstorm with him for a while to

come up with ideas for the letters, then Russ would get all excited and start writing; and we would shut up. **I'd watch him write them, and the whole time, I was thinking, "Man, I want to do that!"** That was back in 1989. **Well, it took me about 10 years before I was any good at what Russ did back then. It took me another 10 years before I was better, and now I'm working on over 20 years of writing copy—and I'm starting to get pretty good at it.** I'm not trying to say I'm great; for what I do, my work is adequate. But I'm proud of what I've accomplished so far, and I know that if I'd given up along the way, I wouldn't *have* that sense of pride.

It took so much work, so much frustration—so many times when I just couldn't take it anymore, when my eyes were so tired and I couldn't write another word, and I was frustrated and confused. I still go through periods like that; in fact, as I write this, **I'm going through one of those periods on another project. I'm in a state of total confusion... but I'll figure it out; I always do.** And I have Chris Lakey to lean on; he helps me co-write this stuff.

Product development is the same way for me. It's still not my strongest area, despite the fact that I've had a hand in developing many hundreds of different products over the years. **I still struggle with it; and I'm still learning, I'm still growing, I'm still going through some confusion. But I don't let that stop me!**

And then there's public speaking. I love listening to a good public speaker. I love it when they're totally in the moment, when they've got the whole crowd in their hands. That's a wonderful thing I've always connected with. **And yet, I was scared of public speaking—terrified of it, in fact!—for years.** Before some of my seminars, I'd spend time in the bathroom throwing up. I'd lose my voice during my talks, sweat profusely, and have to deal with all kinds of anxiety. Sometimes I couldn't sleep the night before—or the week before! Any rational person would have decided, "Your nervous system is trying to tell you something, buddy. Listen to it, because maybe you should choose to do something else besides speak in public." But I really loved it, I wanted to do it, and I pushed myself to do it—and I'm still pushing myself. I'm not the best public speaker; **I've got a million miles to go before I've reached my potential. But I don't let that stop me.**

The same should go for you. You should *not* let any of your limitations stop you. Go for your dreams! Catch your bigger vision! You've *got* to have a bigger vision for yourself. You've got to have something you're going for, something that excites you, something that stimulates you. **Develop a bigger vision for yourself and what you want to accomplish, and then just keep moving forward and dealing with all the pain you encounter along the way.** That's the only way you're ever going to become everything you can possibly become. It's the only way you're ever going to reach your fullest potential. You do the best you can, you continue to grow, and your best continues to get better.

Growth comes from consciously living outside of your comfort zone. **Strictly defined, "growth" means extension. It means taking something from what it was or what it is now and extending it into something else.** Growth in all its forms mean going beyond what you're doing into places you've never been before. In business, this means everything from expanding out of your limited local marketplace to moving beyond your current experiences. If you don't keep doing things on a regular basis that get you outside of your normal existence, you're never going to move beyond that into bigger things.

So the question you must ask yourself is, are you comfortable? Do you accept where you are right now? Because if you're truly satisfied with where you are, then there's no reason for growth—beyond the fact that you might want to challenge yourself. Now, I'm not suggesting that you shouldn't grow, or that it's not a good idea to grow in that case. I'm just saying if you have no goals, and you're exactly where you want to be, and you're pleased with being there, then that would be the *only* reason you wouldn't want to follow this advice. But assuming you don't fit into that category, ask yourself this question: **How do I grow?**

Simple enough. Step outside your comfort level. Live beyond the status quo, beyond what your experiences have been so far.

Of course, that's inherently uncomfortable—which is why most people tend to avoid it at all costs. So you have, on one hand, those who say that they don't want to continue being the way they are; they want growth. People will typically say that they want to be better than they are, that they want to make more money. They want to be more successful than they have been in the past, they want to give more to their favorite charity, they want to do more for society. **People *always* tell you that they want more.**

THINK BIGGER!

And yet, when they look at what it takes to *get* more, all of a sudden there's a breakdown. They may say they want better health, but they're unwilling to diet and exercise. They're unwilling to step on a treadmill. They're unwilling to walk to Wal-Mart instead of driving their car, and they're unwilling to drink 64 ounces of water a day in favor of their Coke. **So most people break down somewhere between their goals and what it actually takes to achieve them.** They shrink back to what's comfortable—what's known to them, what's reassuringly familiar.

What's more, it often takes several trips out of the comfort zone to achieve permanent results. Consider a balloon. When you blow it up and let it go, what happens? After it flies all over the room and eventually runs out of air, it falls on the floor. You go pick it up, and it pretty much looks like that same balloon you started out with. The balloon has regained its original shape. It wasn't stretched to the point of growth by the experience; and when change was applied, it resisted and ultimately rejected it, returning to its "comfort zone," if you will. You can blow it up and release it several times, and it will respond the same way; but eventually, you'll see that the balloon has begun to lose its original shape. It starts trending toward the shape of the expanded balloon you get when you blow it up. The next time you blow it up, you end up with a bigger balloon; if you do that over and over again, eventually you get an even bigger balloon. Now, at some point it will reach a point where you can't blow up it anymore without popping it; but I think you get my point here. **As hard as it may be, as hard as you may resist it, you can keep stepping outside your old comfort zone and achieve bigger results, until you've stabilized into a new comfort zone.**

The reality for most people is that they're so comfortable where they are that they never want to even venture outside of their comfort zone. **Most people live very minimal lives, because deep down, they're happy doing what they do now.** Even if they really want more, they're not willing to do what it takes to achieve more; and even if they do make an effort, they soon shrink back to their original shape. Ultimately, they remove themselves from anything that might challenge them.

But growth is best for us, in the end, even though it might hurt sometimes. This applies to all life experience, not just business growth. **It's those trying times that truly develop a person's character, and bring out the best in them.**

People who avoid challenges never get far, because you can't become a better person by sitting in one place and doing the same things over and over. You've got to continuously do things to grow yourself, to challenge yourself, to get outside your comfort zone, because that's where true growth happens—both on a personal level, and on a business level.

If you want to continue serving the same small marketplace in a limited way, fine. Don't worry about growing or making extra money or even doing a better job for the people you serve, because it's not going to happen. Don't bother reaching out to new marketplaces or trying to develop the kinds of products that might be desired by a larger marketplace. If that little bit of profit is your comfort zone, then so be it. **Or, you can do what it takes to challenge yourself a little—to push beyond what's comfortable, to enter into new marketplaces, to try new things and reap the rewards.**

THINK BIGGER!

Think about pervasive companies like Apple, the ones that don't just try to carve out a bigger slice in an existing marketplace, but step in and create whole new sections of the marketplace that they then dominate. Think about what Apple did to the digital music world when they first invented the iPod. They didn't invent the digital music player, of course; but before the iPod appeared, really good digital music players could hold a few dozen songs at most. The first iPod could hold *thousands*. This transformed how we listen to music, didn't it? Furthermore, it spurred further development of the digital music market. **All this happened because someone said, "We want to push the envelope. We want to go beyond our comfort zone with this device.** We're going to create something that lets people download music in bulk from their computer, and take all that music with them." Today's iPods will hold a storage room full of CDs worth of music.

Now, I remember road trips when you could only take along so many CDs, cassette tapes, or even eight-tracks because you only had so much room to store them. So you had to rummage through your collection and decide what you could afford to take. Then you threw them in your backpack or your briefcase, or maybe you just threw them in a box and put them in the car—and that would be all the music you had available, except for the radio. Well, who hasn't left something they really wanted to listen to at home? Too bad… you'll bring it on the next road trip.

That's no longer necessary; with the iPod, you can take your whole music collection with you. Just connect it into your stereo system, and all your songs are at your fingertips—

160

even those obscure deep cuts from back when you were a kid. You can relive the memories associated with those songs in seconds by finding and listening to them on your iPod. It's not even especially difficult.

The point is, innovation came to the digital music field because Apple stepped up and said, "We're going to push beyond what's normal... beyond what's comfortable." It didn't have to be Apple; any sufficiently determined and innovative electronics company might have done it. **But Apple was the company that took up the challenge, and successfully overcame the existing limits of digital music players.** And, of course, they've done similar things over the years with computers in general, much less products like the iPhone and the iPad. Other companies like Microsoft, Intel, and Dell have driven similar innovation, not just in computing technology but in marketing as well.

We're highly aware of all these companies—and we're buying their products—because they pushed the envelope. They did something that either wasn't normally accepted as being doable, or just hadn't been dreamed up yet. **They continued pushing beyond what was normal into new areas, and they were rewarded for it.**

There's no reason you can't do the same thing.

But most of us are challenged by our small thinking. We're limited by our inability to dream bigger than normal. **Once you put those kinds of fears aside and learn to live beyond your comfort level, your attitude will begin to stretch,** just like that balloon in my earlier analogy. And again, it may not happen the first time, or the second. There may be times when you retreat after an advance, because you're afraid of what's going to happen next. **But if you continue stretching and pushing yourself, you'll find that what was a stretch before becomes the new normal—and then you can stretch yourself even further.**

If you never make that stretch, if you never make any innovative leaps. You'll just continue being who and what you are. You'll continue getting the results you've *been* getting. Not that what you are now is bad; I'm not saying that. But when we're talking about growth, we're talking about becoming bigger and better than before; so even though that may take you beyond your comfort zone, **why not try to stretch to the limits of your God-given talents and abilities?**

For most of us, it just doesn't happen. We all want things to be easy; that's a part of human nature. **But the only real way to make things *easy* is for you to become *stronger*.** That way, you can handle things that other people can't. And I'm not just talking physical strength here; I'm talking about mental and emotional and spiritual as well. **The more skills you have, the more knowledge you've developed, the more talents you've honed, the more you can take on.**

You know, there are some people out there that I call "freaks" because they're so highly driven. They do so much it's just incredible. And yes, some of them *are* abnormal. But mostly, what you see when you look at those people is the outward manifestation of their blur of activity. **What you don't realize is just how massive their goals are. That's part of what's driving them: they have huge goals.** Because they want to accomplish all these things, they've caught that bigger vision for themselves, and they're much more motivated than they would otherwise be.

And another thing: it's not just that they're highly motivated. As I pointed out earlier, **most of these people have surrounded themselves with a lot of really good people.** So they've built a team that provides a synergistic effect when all their efforts are combined. In large part, they're just the front person on the team. **Furthermore, they've developed not just a superior motivation, but superior habits and routines. Those habits and routines help them achieve the results that they enjoy.**

CHAPTER THIRTEEN

**Everybody loves
an offer they perceive
is just for them.**

**The things they want
the most are the things
others cannot get!**

Everyone Loves an Exclusive Offer!

Exclusive offers are very attractive to the average consumer. In fact, **the more a prospect perceives that your offer has been designed with them *specifically* in mind, the more they're going to want it.** Which leads us to a corollary: the things that people want the most are the things that other people can't get. In other words, the more they feel that an offer's intended for just anybody, the less they're likely to want it.

Therefore, **you always have to build something unique into whatever you're selling, in order to draw people in.** The hard part here is that there's nothing that's particularly unique anymore... and there hasn't been, really, for thousands of years. As the Bible puts it, "There's nothing new under the sun." That's part of the Old Testament, so someone pointed that out well before the arrival of Christ himself. Despite this fact—or, perhaps, because of it—**everybody in every marketplace *wants* something new and special.** So if you want to make money with your offers, you have to make your best effort to create such things, so you can differentiate what you're offering from all the similar offers out there.

Here at M.O.R.E., Inc., **the best examples of what I would call exclusive offers—products that fit like a hand to a glove, so that when people get one they say, "This was designed for me"—are our websites.** We've sold millions of dollars worth of "beta tester" promotions since we started developing websites back in the mid-1990s, when the Internet was first taking off. Back then, people might pay $20,000-30,000 for something you can get now for less than $1,000—and often for less than $500. Well, we were one of the very first development companies to offer inexpensive websites to the average consumer. We've specialized in what we call "beta tester" offers, which is where we release a group of websites to testers because they're not quite ready for the marketplace yet—there's always something new that has to be checked out. But we don't release them for free; **we simply give our customers a very special deal on a block of websites.** They're happy because they got them for a low price, and we're happy because we made some money *and* got the bugs worked out of our websites during the testing process.

For example: for many years, we sold different versions of a block of 300 websites to our customers. We were always revising them, making them better, trying new features, and the like. **We'd give our customers 50 of those websites for a phenomenally low price, making it clear that they were getting this deal because these were beta versions that hadn't been tested fully.** We'd tell them we needed beta testers to help us get the bugs out of them—and then we would deliver the sites to them and just blow them away! They would be shocked when they saw what we'd given them; **the quality was high, and the price was a bargain.** Oftentimes we'd throw in a few years of free hosting, too—and all for as little as $9 for all 50 sites, though the price was more likely to be $29 or $39.

No sooner did they get those sites than we'd follow-up

with a special offer, just for them, for an additional block of 250 websites that were similar to the 50 they'd purchased. Our offer pointed out, "Look, you're already a beta tester for our first 50 websites…", and we thanked them profusely. They had a chance to go on the Internet and look over their sites, so we demonstrated to them that we were trustworthy. In all these ways, we proved that our offer was everything that we said it was. They were already sold on the concept of being beta testers for these first 50 websites, so we knew that this custom-tailored offer for an additional 250 websites was the perfect upsell.

This was a true "hand in glove" offer. Now, think about that; because that's how it has to work. Visualize a glove that your hand fits into perfectly. It's wintertime as I'm writing this, and it's very, very cold here in Goessel, Kansas. Most of us who live here don't mind the cold weather…as long as we're dressed for it. So we all wear gloves whenever we go outside. Think about how a nice, well-fitting glove feels, and how warm it keeps your hands. Think of how warm a prospect feels when they fit perfectly into an offer—when it feels like it's been tailored especially for them.

Our beta tester offer was custom-designed just for our existing customers, and it gave them more of what they'd already bought from us. We knew that they were already sold, and it let us speak to that group in a way that let them *know* that the offer was just for them. We've done that with other types of offers, where we try to give our prospects a small piece of the much bigger piece that we want to sell them later. With our websites, that's easy to do.

THINK BIGGER!

In the next few months, we're going to be developing a new offer where we give our beta testers 100 websites to start with, and then we're going to follow up with an offer for an additional 1,000—or maybe even more. We might even start out by giving them 240 websites, and then offer them 2,400 more. **Those kinds of deals just blow people away, because those deals speak directly to what the customers want.** It gives them more of what they already had, and it's exclusive for them.

And remember, the second part of this strategy is that the things people want the most are the things that others can't get. As I write this, we're putting together copy for a new seminar that's coming up in the next month. Over this past weekend, I decided to limit the seminar to just 73 people, each of whom can bring a guest of their choice. Now, why did I do that? Because it made the product super-exclusive. They know that if they're the 74th person to try to sign up, they're not going to get in. It's special—and that's what people really want.

You know, in some ways people are very, very complex; and the smarter they are, the more complicated they are. But in other ways (especially from an emotional standpoint), people are very simple. **Once of the simplicities within the complexity of human behavior is the fact that we all want what other people can't have.** We all want things that are special, created just for us. We all want to feel important; in fact, many of us are *desperate* to feel important. These days, most people don't; they just feel like numbers, or walking wallets. The more you can do to show them how much you appreciate them, that you want to give them access to something very limited, something that other people can't get—the better they'll respond.

We've got another extremely limited offer going at the moment that has a very firm cut-off point. If a prospect misses out on it, then someone else is going to take their position; we're very clear that there are only so many of these positions available. **In a situation like this one, people fight to get in, so they can lock themselves in and not have to worry about somebody else coming along and grabbing that exclusive offer.** That being the case, the profit potential for an offer like this is immense.

These things don't just happen by accident: you have to work to make them special. So how do you accomplish this? By becoming intimately aware of every aspect of the marketplace. As I've emphasized repeatedly in this book, **you must put yourself in the shoes of the people you're trying to reach, and learn every detail you can about them.** What's most important to them? What conversations are going on in their heads, right this moment? How can you strongly communicate your offer in such a way as to make it more desirable?

I just got an email from a man I spent some time with last summer, during our Branson Seminar in Branson, Missouri. He and I had talked about an idea for making millions of dollars back then, and now, months later, he's emailing me with some information on this offer. I've read his email five times—and I still don't understand what the hell he's talking about. He rambled on for three pages and didn't tell me a single thing. He didn't make the offer attractive or exclusive one bit. If it weren't for the fact that I really care about this man, I wouldn't have paid any attention to the offer at all—I would have scrapped it in a second. But instead I'm trying to work with him, trying to go back and forth with him to understand what he's trying to say.

Your offers can't be like that. They have to be crystal clear, so your prospects can instantly see the advantages you've set up for them. **They've got to immediately grasp just how perfect your offer is for them — to perceive, just from looking, that it will fit them like a glove.** To achieve this kind of transparency, you must develop and maintain an intimate awareness of the people you're trying to reach. Learn what's most important to them, and how you can clearly (and I do mean *clearly*) communicate the most important benefits in the shortest period of time, so that they'll instantly see your offer for what it is and will instantly be attracted to it.

It really is amazing how human psychology dominates this equation — how much it feeds into developing effective sales tactics. **You're fighting the tide if you fail to take into account the psychological aspects of business;** the cold math isn't all you need to help you sell your products and opportunities. The exclusivity factor really weighs heavily here, and you can see this when you look at real life examples of how people go about their daily lives and exercise their spending habits. Consider how people respond to any Limited Edition of just about anything. **If they know that only a certain number of a product was made, then all of a sudden the value goes up.** Think of an art print that an artist created only a few hundred copies of; that alone can cause the value to soar. Now, suppose he signed and numbered a select handful of those items. If you have one of those, then your piece of art is even more valuable — simply because there are very few of them available. This kind of exclusivity is what makes most unique art pieces worth more than generic, copied pieces.

When Chris Lakey was a kid, he used to collect baseball and basketball cards. You know, it's one thing just to open a pack of cards, and know that the cards inside are also owned by kids all over the U.S., and that a particular card you're holding is worth a few pennies because it's the same as millions of other cards out there. But usually, some of the cards are available only in limited editions — and you might get lucky. The card company will print on the card pack the odds of what you might pull out of a particular pack of cards. It might be that one out of every 100,000 packs contains an autographed card by whoever happens to be the hottest person in the sport. Chris remembers specifically that back in the early 1990s, Shaquille O'Neal was the hot basketball rookie — and so it was a real thrill to pull a Limited Edition Shaquille O'Neal card. Kids would open dozens of packs of cards trying to get one.

Well, why would you care about any Limited Edition card? **Because it's exclusive.** If you have one, it's likely that no one else you know has one. Chris remembers pulling one of the Limited Edition Shaquille O'Neal cards from a pack once, when he was 15 or 16 years old — and although it wasn't signed, it was worth about $120 at the time. It was just a piece of heavy paper with a picture of a basketball player on it, but the fact that there were only so many of them to go around and *he had one* made him value it more than any old sports card.

His 13-year-old son still has that card stashed somewhere in his room, sealed in a big, heavy piece of protective hard plastic. It's worth ten bucks or so now. But Chris is hoping that one day, that card will become worth something again, and maybe his son can sell it for a little bit of money at some point... or just keep it for the novelty's sake. The point here is that back when it was new, Chris really wanted that card; he wanted all the cards like that. He spent a lot of time and money acquiring meaningless packs of cards to try to find that one Limited Edition card that he knew he wanted the most—**because if he got it, then other people didn't have it. That's the way people are with all kinds of things.**

Similarly, some people like to drive Limited Edition sports cars. If it happens that the manufacturer made only 1,000 of that particular auto, then they're willing to spend more to acquire one. You probably have examples in your own life where you're like that for one thing or another. In our areas of interest or need, we love to get exclusive offers—offers that we perceive are available only to us, or at least to only a few people. **We look for deals that aren't available just anywhere.** We rummage through garage sales looking for that perfect find... that one thing you jump on because no one else can get it, and here it is right in front of you! Let's say you go to the Salvation Army Thrift Store, and you find something they somehow mispriced—something that should have been sold for more. Suddenly, you've scored a good deal on something that isn't available to anybody else—and that makes you feel really good, doesn't it?

That's how your prospects feel when you present them with a perfect fit that you offer for a compelling price. **And it doesn't necessarily have to be a specific item; it could be something more general that lets them know how much you appreciate doing business with them.** Recently, Chris tells me, he received an email from a big electronics chain that said they were having a special after-hours event, and he was invited. Apparently the ad wasn't compelling enough to get him out of his home to drive that half-hour to where the store was located, because he didn't go; but the point is, they *did* extend the invitation to this exclusive event for their "preferred customers." They wanted him to feel special. Now, no doubt they were thronged with people who brought in that little slip from the email that was their ticket to attend the after-hours event... so they could spend money with the store that had made them feel special. In a sense, they all had Golden Tickets that let them get better deals on some items they wanted anyway; and having been made to feel special, do you suppose those people will return and spend more money? Of course they will.

We all want to feel special like that; **so as a marketer, you need to find a way to give your customers and prospects that feeling, so they can appreciate being on the inside.** Nobody wants something that's readily available. Have you ever seen someone wearing a ring with a stone made of coal or sand? Probably not. Nobody wants a sand ring; they want a diamond ring. Why? Because diamonds are rare, and therefore in demand. The cost is high, and a diamond ring is much more exclusive than any plain ring; so people want one. And they don't want just any diamond either, or they would be more likely to accept the inexpensive synthetic ones. No, people want the best natural diamonds possible, diamonds of a high grade, especially those that are naturally colored; those are especially scarce. In other words, people prefer the stones that are genuinely rare, of extraordinarily limited availability.

THINK BIGGER!

Exclusive things make people feel good, which is why you have to carefully evaluate precisely what your customers really, really want the most—and then give it a twist that makes it even more special. What do they feel would be an exclusive buy for them? What do they feel would put them on the inside, put them in the know, or to put them in a position where they can get something that no one else can get? Maybe that's a limited time offer, available to a small group of people, like the one I mentioned earlier. Maybe you find another way to pull out the stops for a preferred group of customers. The point is, you've *got* to come up with that angle that everybody wants, but only a handful can get. People will pay big money for exclusivity; so when you add it to your offers, you'll see your sales will increase.

And one of the things you can do when you're positioning yourself like this is to use what information you have to your advantage. Let's say you know that 10% of your customers are likely to take advantage of your offer, and you have 100 customers (just to have a round number to simplify the math). Well, why not tighten up that offer and make it exclusive to only the first 10 people who respond? Just come right out and say it in your sales copy—and be sure to stick to that number like glue, so you have credibility on your side the next time you do it. **I guarantee that people will respond to that promise of exclusivity.** Set the number wherever you're comfortable. You might even bump it up to 12 or 15, but cut it off when you get there; otherwise, what is your exclusivity worth? **If you're worried about the fact that making something exclusive will limit your profits, then juice up the value some and raise the price.**

And in any case, you'll probably have a lot more than 100 customers to offer something to. For example, we have about 15,000 preferred customers here at M.O.R.E., Inc, and we'll often invite all of them to do business with us or get involved in a new opportunity, a new project, or a new service. **So we're dealing with large numbers; and if in fact only 10% of our customers got involved with us on a particular project, that would be 1,500 people.** Even if we said we were looking for only 200, 300, or 500 people to get involved in something, while that would be a small percentage of our entire group of preferred customers, it's still a lot of people.

The number depends on your model—on what you're looking to accomplish. **But keep in mind that the number needs to be real.** If it's not, if you don't fulfill on your promises or it's obvious that you don't mean what you say, people will figure it out and you'll lose your credibility. **There's no real exclusivity if you say "this offer is only for *this* number of people," and it turns out that it's not.** So make it legit, based on your own numbers and your profit needs. Arrange things so that if you make the offer exclusive to 20 customers, you'll make more money in a week than you've made the entire month before. While you don't need to tell them that, you can't be shy about the number of people involved. **Make sure that they know how exclusive the offer truly is. When played right, this principal works wonderfully well—because it provides you with a psychological edge that most people simply can't resists.** You've made them feel like they've won when they grab that offer, like they've pulled one over on you and their friends and all the other poor slobs who didn't make it in... which means that you win, too. In the end, this can also give you the edge you need to do more business with them.

The important thing to know is that you control the perceptions here, to a large degree—assuming they believe you, or know that they can trust you. You're the one who builds the value; you're the one who builds the exclusivity into your offers, making them more unique, more special, and seemingly less available to everybody else.

Start paying attention to how other marketers are doing this, because it doesn't just happen by accident. You can't just throw crap together and hope people will figure it out, like the guy did who sent me that impenetrable email this morning. As Nathaniel Hawthorne once said, "Easy reading is damn hard writing." **In other words, the more you work on it, the clearer it becomes.** So work hard on your copywriting, and do everything you can to build your offers so that you make your prospects feel special. That's surprisingly rare, as logical as it may seem; **very few marketers bother to make their prospects feel special.**

If you can do that effectively, you'll grab all the customers your competitors aren't getting—and you'll practically mint money.